ALSO BY
FRANCES McCULLOUGH AND BARBARA WITT

*Great Food
Without Fuss*

*Great Feasts
Without Fuss*

*Classic American*

*Food*

*Without Fuss*

# Classic American Food Without Fuss

OUR FAVORITE RECIPES MADE EASY—FINALLY

Frances McCullough
and Barbara Witt

VILLARD
*New York*

*Grateful acknowledgment is made to the following for permission to reprint
previously published material:*

BANTAM BOOKS, A DIVISION OF BANTAM DOUBLEDAY DELL PUBLISHING GROUP, INC.:
Corn Bread recipe from *Hoppin' John's Low County Cooking* by John Martin Taylor.
Copyright © 1992 by John Martin Taylor. Reprinted by permission of
Bantam Books, a division of Bantam Doubleday Dell Publishing Group, Inc.

CHRONICLE BOOKS: Beef Stroganoff recipe from *James McNair's Beef Cookbook* by James McNair,
published by Chronicle Books. Copyright © 1989. Reprinted by permission of
Chronicle Books, San Francisco.

THE ESTATE OF MAGGIE WALDRON: Scampi alla Griglia recipe originally published in
*Fire and Smoke* by Maggie Waldron (101 Productions, 1978). Reprinted by permission
of the Estate of Maggie Waldron.

SUZANNE HAMLIN: Oven Polenta recipe. Reprinted by permission of Suzanne Hamlin.

DAVID HIGHAM ASSOCIATES, LTD: Rice pudding recipe from *English Food* by Jane Grigson
(published by Barrie & Jenkins, an imprint of Random House UK, London). Reprinted by
permission of David Higham Associates Ltd.

ALFRED A. KNOPF, INC., AND MCINTOSH AND OTIS, INC.: Meatball recipe from
*They Called It Macaroni* by Nancy Verde Barr. Copyright © 1990 by Nancy Verde Barr.
Rights throughout the British Commonwealth are administered by McIntosh and Otis, Inc.
Reprinted by permission of Alfred A. Knopf, Inc., and McIntosh and Otis, Inc.

THE LIBERTY BAR: Variation on Virginia Green's Chocolate Cake recipe. Used by permission of the
Liberty Bar, San Antonio, Texas.

LITTLE BROWN AND COMPANY: Black Bean Soup recipe from *American Cookery* by James A. Beard.
Copyright © 1972 by James A. Beard. Reprinted by permission of Little Brown and Company.

SIMON AND SCHUSTER: Lobster Scramble recipe from *Bernard Clayton's Cooking Across America*
by Bernard Clayton. Copyright © 1993 by Bernard Clayton, Jr. Reprinted by permission of
Simon and Schuster.

JAMES VILLAS: Hush Puppies recipe from *My Mother's Southern Kitchen* by James Villas
(Macmillan, 1995). Used by permission of the author.

ISBN: 0-679-44035-6

Random House website address: http://www.randomhouse.com/
Printed in the United States of America on acid-free paper
2 4 6 8 9 7 5 3
First Edition
*Book design by Deborah Kerner*

*A good cook knows when to leave well enough alone.*

Angelo Pellegrini,
*The Unprejudiced Palate*

# Acknowledgments

As usual, our cook friends have been more than generous with their advice and counsel, which have improved this book enormously. We're indebted to Jo Bettoja, JoAnn Clevenger, Shirley Corriher, Susan Costner, Suzanne Hamlin, Diana Kennedy, Deborah Madison, John Taylor, Sylvia Thompson, Eileen Weinberg, Faith Willinger, Paula Wolfert, and Lisa Yockelson.

# Contents

# Introduction

The classics, the simplest, the best—we've set ourselves a big challenge here. Who are we to say what's the best, never mind the simplest, when even what's classic is a big question? We have to admit that recipes that scream "best ever" set our teeth on edge, and the cookbooks that offer "the best" of anything immediately get our backs up—but here we are, joining them. And we're joining a crowd: Cooking magazines are routinely reinventing the wheel, testing dozens upon dozens of similar recipes for a single dish to find "the best," and a number of the recipes in this book have entire cookbooks devoted to them, from brownies to cheesecake to chicken soup.

So who needs this book? We do, for starters. As with all our no-fuss cookbooks, this approach solves a problem for us. It had its genesis when one of us was revisiting corn bread and hauled out all her big old classic cookbooks, only to find a bewildering number of options. Which was the best? Which was the easiest? Both of us had favorite corn breads, but they didn't answer the question. We didn't want even *more* recipes, we didn't want an entire book on corn bread, we just wanted the easiest, best recipe.

The more we explored this subject, the more sure we became that we weren't alone. The less time we have, the more sophisticated we become about taste, and the further removed we are from succeeding generations of cooks who know their way around the kitchen, the more we need an instant sourcebook. Here it is: the single book you need on your shelf when you have to come up with a great chocolate cake in a hurry.

The best? Of course we haven't made or tasted every version of every classic dish, so we're sure we're missing some good bets. But we've done our homework, looked in all the best cookbooks as well as a number of obscure ones that yielded some little treasures; we've asked the best cooks we know, some of whom are famous chefs, for their opinions and their little tricks for making dishes simpler or tastier, and we've cooked ourselves silly in the course of tracking down what seems to us the best. And we've kept a priority in mind: taste. If a little more work will make a big difference in flavor, we tell you and give you the option of a little more fuss. Some dishes just can't be simplified without losing their character, and in those cases we've stuck to the best, period. In the end, of course, it's just our opinion—but isn't that what you wanted?

We thought long and hard about what's a classic. The definition we came up with is dishes that were standard in cookbooks of about 1960—and that we still want to eat today. Part of what's so comforting about comfort food is that it's classic, satisfying, and familiar. So these are *our* favorites, and we hope you'll find your own favorites among them.

What's a classic depends a little on location. In Italy no one has heard of spaghetti and meatballs, and plenty of sophisticated American cooks happily cook up polenta but would never think of making cornmeal mush, even though they're exactly the same—a gift to Italy from the New World. And of course no classic dish is written in stone—recipes evolve in the same way everything else does, and if something's an improvement, great; if not, let's go back to the best version we have.

Why would you want to make these old recipes when you can be cooking the latest recipes from the hottest chefs—tall food, fusion cuisine, exotica flown in from all over the globe? We like to play with those things too, but in the end there's a reason classics are classics. As one famous food writer we know said recently, "I don't want to eat any more *interesting* food." Watch your dinner guests' faces when they realize they're going to have a great beef stew for dinner—what a relief! There's a real joy in eating well-prepared dishes with character and personal history, the joy of the excellent and familiar.

Most of all we hope you'll rediscover some old favorites for yourself—real cream of tomato soup from scratch, a truly sensational cheesecake—and make them part of your repertoire. The satisfaction of making real food with a minimum of fuss on your part can hardly be overestimated. And it's simply amazing how often the simplest version really is the best, as we've discovered to our great delight.

# A Note on Ingredients

Throughout this book we call for specific ingredients, sometimes by brand name when the product is exemplary and we think using it contributes to the success of the dish. We recommend keeping these ingredients on hand.

- Hellmann's mayonnaise (Best Foods west of the Rockies)
- Muir Glen canned organic tomatoes (natural foods stores and some supermarkets)
- Wondra instant flour, a granulated flour that dissolves quickly
- Boyajian citrus oils (Williams-Sonoma, Dean and DeLuca, and specialty food stores)
- Colman's dry mustard
- canned chicken broth
- Parmesan cheese, by which we mean real Parmigiano-Reggiano
- pure vanilla extract, especially Neilsen-Massey (Williams-Sonoma, Dean and DeLuca, and specialty food stores)
- salt (we prefer sea salt or kosher salt)
- nutmeg (we greatly prefer freshly grated)
- Chatham Village garlic croutons

Starters

# Stuffed Mushrooms

*M*ushrooms stuffed with what?" you might well ask. There are cheese-stuffed, ham-stuffed, clam-stuffed, spinach-stuffed, self-stuffed, and even stuffing-stuffed. The very idea of stuffed mushrooms makes epicures hum. Even when we could buy only cultivated ones, we all loved mushrooms. We sliced them into salads, dipped them from crudité baskets, baked them into pizza toppings, and tossed them into soups and stews. Now we can buy a variety of sublime exotic mushrooms, both fresh and dried. Here are four splendid stuffings to remind you why stuffed mushrooms are an American favorite.

*Serves 6*

### Clam-Stuffed Mushrooms

18 large mushrooms, tough stem ends
    removed

1/4 cup olive oil

2 tablespoons fresh lemon juice

3 garlic cloves, minced

3 shallots, minced

3 strips of bacon, fried crisp, drained,
    and crumbled, drippings reserved

2 6 1/2-ounce cans chopped clams,
    drained

1/4 cup chopped drained jarred
    roasted red peppers

1 tablespoon Worcestershire sauce

1/4 teaspoon cayenne pepper, or more
    to taste

1/4 cup fine dry bread crumbs

1/4 cup minced parsley

1/4 cup freshly grated Parmesan
    cheese

Brush the mushrooms clean and mince the tender stems. Mix the olive oil and lemon juice and dip each cap into the mixture, reserving any leftover oil and lemon juice. Turn the caps filling side down on a broiler rack and broil about 3 inches from the heat until they're half cooked but still firm. Sauté the garlic and shallots in the bacon drippings until soft. Drain. Mix the stems, bacon, garlic, shallots, clams, peppers, Worcestershire, and cayenne. Mound the stuffing into the mushrooms and top with the bread crumbs mixed with parsley, Parmesan, and reserved oil and lemon juice. Broil the stuffed mushrooms about 3 inches from the heat for a couple of minutes, until the crumbs are crisp and golden and the filling is hot.

HAM-STUFFED MUSHROOMS: *Prepare the mushrooms as directed. Make the filling with ¼ pound cubed ham, minced in a food processor (about ½ cup), a rounded teaspoon of Dijon mustard, ¼ teaspoon dried oregano, and 2 tablespoons each minced green bell pepper and shallot, sautéed until soft in a little garlic oil. Top each cap with a small strip of fontina cheese and broil until melted.*

MUSHROOMS STUFFED WITH SWISS CHARD: *Prepare the mushrooms as directed. Make the filling by rolling and cutting red Swiss chard leaves into very thin ribbons, then stir-frying them in garlic oil for about 10 minutes. Drain well, blot with paper towels, and run a chef's knife back and forth through the chard to mince it. Return it to the dry skillet and add a dash of liquid smoke, salt and freshly ground pepper, and just enough heavy cream to coat the chard. Top each stuffed cap with a dusting of Parmesan and broil.*

STUFFED RAW MUSHROOMS: *Cream together ½ cup each of crumbled French Roquefort or Danish or Maytag blue cheese and fully ripe French*

Camembert. Blend in ½ cup ground walnuts, 1 teaspoon Worcestershire sauce, and ½ teaspoon curry powder. Pipe the mixture from a pastry bag (or cut the corner tip from a plastic freezer bag) into raw mushroom caps dipped in lemon juice to keep them white. Serve chilled.

➤ Create your own stuffings and serve them as a side dish with roasts or grilled fish. With a ground meat and bread stuffing, portobellos can be a main course.

# Gravlax

*L*ess rich tasting than smoked salmon, this Scandinavian delicacy has become popular with American cooks because it's so easy to salt-cure in home refrigerators. It makes a splendid addition to a company buffet; serve it with a piquant mustard-dill sauce and thinly sliced rye bread triangles. Gravlax can be made up to a week in advance.

*Serves 10 to 12 generously*

1 large bunch of fresh dill, heavy
    stems removed
⅓ cup kosher salt
½ cup sugar
2 teaspoons coarsely ground white
    pepper

¼ cup cognac
2 center-cut salmon fillets, skinned
    and boned (2 pounds finished
    weight)
Mustard-Dill Sauce (recipe follows)

Use a shallow ceramic or stainless-steel container big enough to hold the fillets one on top of the other. You'll also need a heavy weight to fit inside the container, like a cutting board or plate weighted with a heavy can. Put half of the dill fronds on the bottom of the dish. Mix the salt, sugar, pepper, and cognac together and rub the marinade into both sides of the fillets. Lay one fillet on top of the dill. Add the rest of the dill and sandwich on the second fillet. Weight the salmon as evenly as possible. On a cold, but not freezing, winter day you can cure it outside or on the porch—otherwise, put it in the refrigerator for 48 hours, turning and draining the fillets every 12 hours and keeping them properly weighted. Slice thinly on the bias and serve with Mustard-Dill Sauce.

*An alternative sauce: sour cream mixed with chopped cilantro, minced pickled jalapeño pepper, and scallions.*

*Keep the gravlax in the refrigerator, wrapped securely in foil, for up to 1 week.*

## Mustard-Dill Sauce

Mix ½ cup dark mustard with 2 teaspoons Colman's dry mustard, ¼ cup sugar, ¼ cup rice vinegar, ½ cup safflower oil, and ½ cup minced fresh dill. It makes about 1¼ cups.

# Quiche Lorraine

*Q*uiche holds a favored place on any list of American classics. Not the mile-high junk food quiche—the butt of all those jokes—but the pure, luxuriously simple, and soul-satisfying quiche lorraine, which dates all the way back to the 16th century. Now that there are good frozen pastry shells on the market, you can prepare quiche on a whim, and the tart shells are just the right size for accompanying a big mixed salad or starting off a company dinner.

*Serves 6*

6 frozen 3-inch tart shells or a 9-inch
  pie shell, preferably Oronoque
  Orchards
4 large eggs
6 strips of bacon, fried crisp, drained,
  and crumbled

1¼ cups heavy cream
salt and freshly ground black pepper
freshly grated nutmeg to taste

Partially bake the tart shells according to package instructions or line the shells with a generous sheet of parchment paper, filling the bottom with dried beans, and bake in a preheated 400° oven for about 10 minutes or until the pastry shrinks away from the sides of the pan. Remove the parchment and beans (save them to use again) and return the shells to the oven for another 5 minutes or until they take on a pale golden hue. Lower the heat to 375°, then quickly paint the bottom of the shells with one of the eggs, lightly beaten, to seal the crust from the custard. Divide the bacon bits among the shells. Whisk together the remaining eggs, cream, salt, pepper, and nutmeg. Pour the custard into the shells. Bake for 20 to 25 minutes until golden brown and set. Let cool slightly before serving.

*You can make a good Alsatian onion tart by slowly sautéing 2 thinly sliced medium white onions in 3 tablespoons butter until they're very soft but not brown. Season the onions with salt, pepper, and a pinch of cayenne. Dust them with a little instant flour (such as Wondra), toss, and cool. Divide the onions among the tart shells and fill them with custard. Bake as directed.*

## Fried Cheese

*There's Greek saganaki (kasseri), Yugoslav pohani sir (Gruyère), Norwegian tre kokker (Camembert), Italian fried mozzarella . . . and then some. They're all molten chunks of cheese perfect for—in this order—a jolting jigger of ouzo or lemon, a side of sautéed cherry tomatoes, lingonberries, a spicy marinara, or just a bed of dressed greens. The secret to a crusty fried cheese is a meticulous coating of egg and dry bread crumbs mixed with a little flour. Fork-beat an egg with a splash of water or milk and dip in ½-inch slices of cheese, moistening all sides and ends. Dip into the crumb mixture, coating every surface. Let dry on a cake rack. Repeat the dipping and coating. Dry again or refrigerate uncovered. Fry the cheese in 1¼ inches of hot oil, turning once and draining on paper towels when golden and crisp. Other cheeses to use for their smooth-melting qualities are Danish fontina and Monterey Jack.*

# New Orleans–Style Shrimp Rémoulade

*I*t's amazing how convoluted dishes can become in their journey to our tables. When you think of how many thousands of hands have labored over them and how often they've been passed from cook to cook in foreign languages, it's miraculous they survive at all. *Sauce rémoulade* left France as a simple mustard and herb mayonnaise with a few capers and minced gherkins and resurfaced in New Orleans with a far more complex and assertive personality. Although it can also accompany cold meat and fish, rémoulade is the ideal sauce or dip for spicy chilled shrimp, a classic New Orleans dish.

*Serves 4 to 6*

## The Shrimp:

1 12-ounce bottle light beer

2 garlic cloves, peeled and crushed

¼ teaspoon cayenne pepper

1 pound (24 to 36) large fresh shrimp

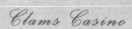

## *Clams Casino*

*This classic starter can also be made with oysters. Sauté 4 minced slices of bacon with ½ cup minced shallot and ¼ cup each minced celery and red and green bell pepper. When the vegetables are soft and the bacon crisp, drain off the fat and squeeze ½ lemon over them. Add a dash or two of both Worcestershire and Tabasco sauce. Spoon over the clams or oysters in individual ramekins or shells and broil about 3 inches from the heat for about 4 minutes.*

*8*

CLASSIC AMERICAN FOOD WITHOUT FUSS

### The Rémoulade Sauce:

1½ cups mayonnaise, preferably
  Hellmann's (light is fine)

2 garlic cloves, pressed

1 tablespoon Creole mustard

1 tablespoon tomato paste

1 tablespoon fresh lemon juice

1 tablespoon anchovy paste (optional)

1 rounded tablespoon grated
  horseradish, preferably fresh

½ teaspoon Tabasco sauce or
  to taste

¼ teaspoon salt

1 tablespoon paprika

pinch of cayenne pepper

1 teaspoon dry mustard, preferably
  Colman's

¼ cup minced parsley

¼ cup minced scallions or chives

### To Serve:

shredded romaine lettuce

lemon wedges

Put the beer, garlic, and cayenne in a 2-quart saucepan, bring to a boil, and reduce the heat to simmer gently for 5 minutes. Add the shrimp and bring the liquid back to a boil, letting the shrimp cook for only 30 seconds more. Drain the shrimp and let them cool, then peel and devein them.

Whisk all of the sauce ingredients together and chill.

Make a bed of the romaine on each plate and divide the shrimp among them. Completely cover the shrimp with the sauce and garnish with lemon wedges.

*Use Dijon mustard if Creole mustard is unavailable, but the flavor will be less distinctive.*

*Other common sauce ingredients are minced capers, fresh tarragon, celery, and sour gherkins.*

# Shrimp Toast

*I*f you've never made the real thing at home, this recipe will be a delightful revelation. Shrimp toast isn't just a festive appetizer; it's also a delicious companion to a main-dish soup, a vegetable stir-fry, or a perfect addition to a buffet table—the hot toasts will keep for about 30 minutes.

### Makes 24 small squares or 12 triangles

6 slices of day-old bread, crusts
   removed
½ pound medium shrimp, peeled
2 quarter-size slices of fresh ginger,
   smashed and minced
2 garlic cloves, smashed and minced
2 scallions, including some of the
   green, minced
salt and freshly ground pepper to taste

1 large egg, lightly beaten
1 tablespoon cornstarch
2 tablespoons sherry, sake, or rice
   wine
8 canned water chestnuts, rinsed and
   minced
peanut oil for deep frying
sesame seeds
cilantro leaves for garnish

Cut each slice of bread into 4 quarters or 2 triangles and spread them out to dry for a couple of hours so the bread won't absorb too much oil. If you can't wait, tuck the bread into a low-temperature toaster oven or dry the slices in a microwave. Put the shrimp, ginger, garlic, scallions, salt and pepper, egg, cornstarch, and sherry into a food processor and mince to a smooth thick paste. Stir in the water chestnuts. Heat 1½ inches of oil in a wok or sauté pan to 350° on a deep fry thermometer or until bubbles gather around a wooden chopstick held upright in the middle of the pan. Spread the paste generously on the bread, mounding it in the center. Dip the tops in the sesame seeds. Drop the toast upside down into the hot oil and cook for about 1½ minutes on each side. The toast should be dark golden brown. Drain well on paper

## Buffalo Chicken Wings

*Here's another palate-tingling dish often compromised by poor preparation and confusion over which sauce goes with what. The chicken wings take the hot sauce, and the cool celery scoops up the blue cheese dip. Here's all there is to it: Buy a bottle of Crystal Hot Wing Sauce. Fry the plump chicken wings in shallow hot oil until partially cooked, about 5 minutes. Drench them in the hot sauce and finish them under the broiler. Salt them and, if you like them hotter, sprinkle lightly with cayenne. The celery ribs must be juicy, crisp, and cold. For the dip, add a dash of white vinegar to a minced clove of garlic and 5 chopped, trimmed scallions, ½ cup mayonnaise, ¼ cup sour cream, and room-temperature blue cheese to taste, mashed in with a fork. Presto! Bring on the iced beer.*

towels and serve with the cilantro leaf garnish. Shrimp toasts will stay warm in a low oven for up to 30 minutes if you're making the recipe in batches. You can also reheat them in a 400° oven for about 5 minutes.

*If you eschew the very thought of frying in oil, try baking the toasts in a 350° oven until they're golden. A light top-brushing of peanut or sesame oil is a reasonable compromise. They can also be broiled.*

*The shrimp paste is almost endlessly useful: Form leftover paste into 1-inch balls and freeze them. Without defrosting, they can be steamed or deep-fried with a light cornstarch or fine crumb coating and dipped in your favorite Asian sauce. If steamed, they can be floated on soup or stir-fried with mixed vegetables. Deep-fried, try them in a sweet and sour sauce with squares of green bell pepper and chunks of fresh pineapple for a perfect supper with vegetable fried rice. Press the thawed shrimp balls into stemmed shiitake mushrooms or red bell pepper boats and broil them for canapés. You can also tuck* some shrimp paste into a wonton wrapper, fold into a triangle sealed with egg wash, then deep-fry until crisp and golden.

≈ There's no reason you couldn't substitute raw salmon for the shrimp. Use minced fresh dill to season the paste and minced fennel instead of water chestnuts. A touch of hot-sweet mustard would give the mixture some depth.

≈ There are several delicious ways to vary the flavor and character of shrimp toast:

- Add grated lime zest, minced cilantro, and a squirt of chili sauce to the mixture.
- Add minced ham or cooked bacon bits.
- Season the mixture with curry powder and dip the tops into unsweetened coconut instead of sesame seeds.
- Spread a thin film of wasabi paste on the bread before adding the shrimp paste.

---

≈

### Guacamole

This favorite dip also works as a refreshing, delightfully textured condiment for all kinds of seasoned grilled dishes. Press a little coarse salt into a tablespoon of minced onion with a fork. Roughly mash a dead-ripe Hass avocado against the side of the bowl, and mix with the salted onion. Fold in a rounded tablespoon of chopped cilantro and a minced ½ jalapeño pepper. Sprinkle 3 tablespoons seeded and minced ripe tomato over the top. You may want to add a big squeeze of fresh lime juice.

---

# Coquille Saint-Jacques

his is actually not a dish, just the French name for the scallops found off the coast of Brittany and prepared in various ways. We can't remember anyone ever preparing at home what was a most popular menu item in the fancy Continental restaurants of the fifties, probably because the scallop, common in some coastal regions, was considered a national delicacy and their availability in retail seafood markets was limited. This is a simple, elegant, do-ahead company first course that everyone will savor.

*Serves 6*

1 pound bay scallops

flour

salt and freshly ground pepper to taste

4 tablespoons (½ stick) butter

1 garlic clove, smashed and peeled
   (see page 112)

4 shallots, minced

pinch of cayenne pepper

¼ cup dry vermouth or dry white wine

1½ cups heavy cream, preferably not
   ultrapasteurized

6 tablespoons grated Parmesan
   cheese

Drain and blot the scallops dry. Dust very lightly with flour from a strainer or hand sifter and shake off the excess. Salt and pepper the scallops. Heat the butter and garlic in a large nonstick skillet over medium heat until the butter is fragrant. Remove the garlic, increase the heat to high, and add the scallops without allowing them to touch; cook them in 2 batches if necessary. Shake the pan, rolling the scallops around until they're golden. Transfer them to a bowl with a slotted spoon and keep warm.

Soften the shallots in the butter remaining in the skillet. Add the cayenne, pour in the wine, and let it sizzle down by half while you scrape up the bottom of the pan. Add the cream and boil to reduce the sauce to a thick coating consistency, 5 to 10 minutes. Add salt and pepper. Add the scallops and coat them well. Divide among individual scallop shells or ramekins and dust the tops with the Parmesan cheese. When ready to serve, slide under the broiler to reheat and brown the tops.

    ✐ *These scallops can be made early in the day and stored, covered with plastic wrap, in the refrigerator until ready to broil and serve.*

    ✐ *To serve this dish as a main course, add the Parmesan to the cream sauce and serve the scallops on 2 toast triangles with a mound of stir-fried fresh spinach in between. A few toasted pine nuts make a nice garnish.*

    ✐ *To lighten the dish, add strips of Italian plum tomatoes to the skillet with just a dash of cream and top the ramekins with a little grated Parmesan or fontina to melt under the broiler.*

# Deviled Eggs

*N*ow that eggs have been decriminalized, we're free to enjoy these scrumptious morsels again. If you think no one's been missing them, just try putting out a platter of them at your next party—they're guaranteed to be the first thing to disappear.

    You have a lot of options with deviled eggs: They can lie on their backs (when the eggs are cut lengthwise) or stand up straight (cut crosswise, with a slice taken off each tapered end so they'll stay upright). The reclining egg is the one you want if you have one of those yard-sale deviled egg plates; the upright one is easier to deal with at a cocktail party. You can make them with mayonnaise or soft butter or a combination. You can season them with Worcestershire, Dijon mustard, dry mustard (our favorite), or curry, and you can add everything from ham bits to capers.

You don't want very fresh eggs here because they'll be harder to peel, but that shouldn't be a problem unless you live on a farm; supermarket eggs weren't born yesterday.

*Serves 12*

1 dozen extra-large eggs at room
   temperature
6 tablespoons mayonnaise
   (preferably Hellmann's), or soft
   butter, or a mixture

1 tablespoon Worcestershire sauce
   (optional)
½ teaspoon dry mustard, preferably
   Colman's, or more to taste
salt and freshly ground pepper to taste
paprika (optional)

Put the eggs in a saucepan just large enough to hold them, cover with cold water, and slowly bring to a boil. Once the water boils, cover the saucepan and take it off the heat. Let stand for 15 minutes to cook the eggs. Put the pan in the sink and run cold water over the eggs (the Germans call this procedure "frightening the eggs"—it helps to loosen the shells). Once the eggs are suitably terrified, tap them

---

### *Hummus bi Tahini*

*The superb Middle Eastern dip for torn chunks of pita bread also works as a topping for grilled fish. Rinse, drain, and puree 2 (1-pound) cans of chickpeas in a food processor, then add 2 to 3 rounded tablespoons of tahini (sesame paste), 1 tablespoon at a time. Season the mixture with pressed garlic, fresh lemon juice, salt, and pepper. It should be quite tart and garlicky with the consistency of fluffy mayonnaise. If it's too thick, thin it with water. Serve hummus drizzled generously with olive oil mixed with paprika and a sprinkle of minced parsley if you have it.*

---

against the side of the pan all over to crack the shells. Let them sit in the cold water until you're ready to peel them.

Cut the cooked peeled eggs in half and transfer the yolks to a small bowl. Mash them well with a fork and add the mayonnaise and seasonings. Stuff the egg whites with the filling and finish them with a shake of paprika if you like.

Wrap the egg plate loosely in plastic wrap and refrigerate for at least an hour before serving. Decorate the plate with sprigs of watercress or parsley.

➤ *You'll notice these aren't hard-boiled eggs. Anytime you're dealing with protein you want to avoid boiling it, or the food will toughen. And in the case of eggs, you can get a nasty-looking greenish-black ring around the yolks as well if you boil them. This method avoids all that, and besides, it's easier.*

➤ *You can put the filling ingredients in a zipper plastic bag and mush them thoroughly together with your fingers—then just snip off a corner and neatly pipe out the filling into the egg white.*

➤ *For an onion flavor, add snipped chives or minced scallions.*

➤ *If plain old deviled eggs seems too pedestrian, finish them off with a dollop of caviar or mix in some chopped smoked salmon.*

Soups

# Gazpacho

*E*ven in Spain, the national home of this delectable soup, there are dozens of ways to make it. In America sometimes things like Worcestershire sauce get added, but as usual, we think the simplest version tastes best.

*Serves 6*

3 slices of stale Italian or French or
    country bread
2 tablespoons red wine vinegar or
    sherry vinegar
2 cups cold water
2 garlic cloves, smashed and peeled
    (see page 112)
1 small cucumber, peeled, seeded,
    and roughly chopped

2 pounds tomatoes, roughly chopped
2 green bell peppers, roughly chopped
1 large red onion, roughly chopped
2 tablespoons extra-virgin olive oil
1 cup tomato juice, preferably organic,
    or V-8
salt to taste

In a small bowl, soak the bread, vinegar, and garlic cloves in the water for a few minutes. Mince a quarter of each of the chopped vegetables and set aside in small bowls for the garnish.

In a blender, puree the bread mixture, remaining vegetables, olive oil, and tomato juice, adding more cold water as needed to make a creamy thick soup. Taste for salt and adjust seasoning. Cover the soup and refrigerate it for at least an hour. Serve chilled, passing the bowls of garnishes at the table.

*If you don't add the onion until an hour or two before serving, you can pre-pare the soup a day or two ahead (otherwise the onion tends to make the soup ferment). You can also use scallions instead of onion.*

✐ Do not add ice cubes to the gazpacho, as many recipes recommend; it dilutes the flavor and often contributes an unpleasant off taste as well.

✐ Another very welcome garnish is little bread dice, fried in sizzling olive oil just before serving the soup.

# Minestrone

*O*f all the thousands of beloved minestrone recipes, this one emerges as simple, deeply flavored, and flexible. It's adapted from the notes of Angelo Pellegrini, an Italian-born English professor who settled on the West Coast and whose fresh-from-the-garden cooking became an inspiration to great cooks like M.F.K. Fisher and Alice Waters.

This is minestrone without the usual sweetness of carrots, peas, and string beans. Pellegrini cautions against throwing everything in the refrigerator into the soup or letting it cook for hours or offering it without some condiment to bring up the flavor—what he calls "sauce" here. But he acknowledges that people have idiosyncratic ideas about their minestrone—thick enough to stand a spoon in or thinned into a relatively light soup. Your call.

*Serves 8*

2 quarts water

1 small ham hock

2 10-ounce packages frozen tiny lima beans

coarsely cut vegetables as desired: ½ head of savoy cabbage, ½ bunch of Swiss chard, 3 medium zucchini, diced, 4 celery ribs, diced, plus some chopped inner celery leaves

salt to taste

**The "Sauce":**

¼ *pound finely minced salt pork or pancetta*

½ *medium onion, finely chopped*

*4 garlic cloves, finely chopped*

*1 14.5-ounce can Muir Glen diced tomatoes, or 2 large fresh tomatoes, coarsely chopped, including the juice*

*pinch of ground allspice*

*freshly ground pepper to taste*

**To Finish and Serve:**

*handful of small pasta such as macaroni, penne, or ditalini, cooked al dente, optional*

¼ *cup minced fresh basil*

*grated Parmesan cheese for serving*

In a large kettle or dutch oven, bring the water to a boil with the ham hock and beans. Lower the heat and simmer uncovered for an hour. Remove the ham hock and save for another use. Puree the beans and broth in a blender or use a hand blender and puree in the pot.

Meanwhile, prepare the sauce: In a saucepan over low heat, fry the salt pork gently without browning it too much. If you're using pancetta, sauté it in a little olive oil. Add the onion and garlic and continue cooking until the mixture is very slightly browned. Add the tomatoes and their juice, season with allspice and pepper, and simmer gently for about 45 minutes.

Add the vegetables to the broth and let them cook, uncovered, over medium heat for 15 to 20 minutes, until they're very slightly cooked. Taste for seasoning and salt to taste.

Add the sauce to the soup along with the pasta. Cook over medium heat for 5 minutes and add the basil just a couple of minutes before serving, stirring it into the soup.

Ladle the soup into bowls and pass the Parmesan at the table.

*Pellegrini doesn't recommend serving salad with the soup—just following it with fruit.*

*For a speedier version, you can start with the sauce, doubling the quantity. Add a spoonful of minced fresh thyme and a handful of parsley and celery. Cut savoy cabbage or chard directly into the sauce and add as much boiling water as you need for the consistency you want. Salt to taste and add pasta or not, as you please. Finish the soup with a can of black bean soup and the basil.*

# Cream of Tomato Soup

A surprising number of people have never tasted fresh cream of tomato soup—which is too bad, considering how terrific it is. It's also easy to make from scratch, using either canned tomatoes or fresh dead-ripe ones. We usually use canned, since we think of cream of tomato soup when the weather gets chilly and tomatoes are out of season. But take care in choosing your canned tomatoes; our favorites are organic Muir Glen diced tomatoes, which work perfectly here.

*Serves 6*

2 tablespoons butter

1 tablespoon olive or safflower oil

3 large shallots, chopped

2 14.5-ounce cans Muir Glen diced tomatoes or 3 pounds fresh tomatoes, peeled, seeded, and chopped, with juice

1/4 teaspoon dried thyme leaves or 3/4 teaspoon fresh

2 cups homemade (page 25) or canned chicken broth

1/4 teaspoon baking soda

1/2 teaspoon sugar

1/2 cup heavy cream

pinch of cayenne pepper (optional)

salt and freshly ground pepper to taste

fresh basil leaves for garnish (optional)

In a 2-quart saucepan, melt the butter and oil together over medium heat. Add the shallots and cook slowly for about 10 minutes or until soft. Add the tomatoes, thyme, and chicken broth, bring to a simmer, and stew slowly, covered, for about 20 minutes.

Turn off the heat and puree the soup in the pan using a hand blender. (Or pour it into a blender, in batches, to puree—be careful; hot soup can spurt out of the blender jar, so use a kitchen towel to cover the top and keep your hand firmly on it.)

Add the baking soda, sugar, cream, and cayenne. Heat the soup for serving, but don't let it boil. Taste for seasoning and serve in warmed soup bowls. Grind some pepper on top and add a few snips of fresh basil if available. Minced lemon zest with parsley is another delicious option.

*You can also make this unusual cream of green tomato soup. Cut up 3 large onions and cook them slowly in 4 tablespoons butter in a large heavy pot. When they're soft, add 10 big green tomatoes, cored but not peeled, cut up. Cook slowly for 30 minutes, until the tomatoes are soft. Cover the pot and cook for 30 minutes more. Add 1 cup chicken broth. Pass the soup through a strainer to extract the seeds and skin. (Now you have the base of the soup, which can be frozen.) For each 2 cups base, add 1½ cups half-and-half, 2 teaspoons sugar, and 1 teaspoon salt. Taste for seasoning; the sugar and salt balance is crucial here. Serve hot or chilled, topped with a tablespoon of sour cream.*

# Chicken Soup

*C*hicken soup at its best is the ultimate comfort food. It can also be watery, almost flavorless, not worth eating. How do you steer around that kind of chicken soup?

This version is particularly rich because it starts off with chicken broth instead of water.

Chicken soup cognoscenti claim that an aluminum pot will contribute an off taste to the soup, as will using a wooden spoon, which inevitably holds flavors from previous cooking projects. To be safe, they say, use a stainless-steel or enameled cast-iron pot and a metal spoon.

Very important: Keep the soup at a simmer; boiling it will produce a nasty taste. Try using a Flame-Tamer.

*Serves 6*

1 large chicken, about 5 pounds, cut up, plus neck and giblets (but not the liver)

extra chicken thighs and wings for extra flavor (optional)

1 quart canned chicken broth

1 celery rib plus a few of the yellow leaves

2 parsley sprigs

1 large bay leaf

4 garlic cloves

2 leeks, thoroughly cleaned and split, or 1 medium onion, quartered

2 fresh thyme sprigs or 1 teaspoon dried

salt to taste

5 to 10 peppercorns to taste

2 cloves

1 large carrot, roughly chopped

snipped fresh herbs such as parsley, dill, and chives for garnish (optional)

Place the chicken pieces and giblets in a large heavy soup pot and add chicken broth to cover, adding water if you need more liquid. Put the lid on the pot and bring it to a boil. Remove the lid and lower the heat so the liquid simmers, skimming off any foam. Once the foam stops rising, add the remaining ingredients, starting out with ½ teaspoon salt.

Cook the soup, uncovered, adding water as needed to keep the chicken submerged, at a steady simmer for 2 to 2½ hours, until the meat is nearly falling off the bones. Remove the chicken; when it's cool enough to handle, take the meat off the bones. Shred the chicken and set aside. Strain the soup and discard the vegetables, which will have given their all to the soup. Add the chicken pieces back to the soup and taste for seasoning.

If you like, you can add more vegetables: diced carrots, celery, mushrooms, peas, cooked potatoes, chopped leeks, etc. Sauté them in a little butter before adding them to the soup. Cooked rice, egg noodles, and pastina are other delicious additions.

Serve the soup very hot in warmed soup bowls, sprinkled with parsley or dill if you like.

➤ *Be wary of adding too many root vegetables; a lot of carrots or parsnips will add too much sweetness, and stronger-flavored roots like celeriac will overwhelm the soup. Some recipes suggest adding the skin of an onion for color, but it will also add bitterness.*

➤ *It's a little extra fuss, but if you want the best flavor, brown the chicken pieces first in a touch of butter before adding them to the pot.*

➤ *Don't toss out the chicken gizzards; the liver will turn the soup bitter, but the gizzards deliver a lot of excellent flavor. They're the small hard bits in the innards package.*

➤ *The chicken will have given a great deal of its flavor to the broth. If you want to use it for another purpose—salad or potpie—remove the breasts and thighs after 30 minutes of cooking and just return the bones and skin to the pot.*

➤ *For a Mexican version, top the filled soup bowls with avocado dice, chopped cilantro, a minced jalapeño, and a few strips of toasted tortilla. If you have any chipotle chili paste around, stir in a spoonful.*

*Try this variation on Southern cook Edna Lewis's technique for producing a delectable chicken broth without fuss: Cut up 4 chicken thighs into 1-inch pieces, leaving the central bone intact—or cut it in half if you can. Chicken wings are good here too; cut them into thirds. Dice an onion. Heat a dutch oven over high heat and, when it's very hot, add the chicken pieces and onion. Season with salt and pepper, stir briskly for 5 minutes, then cover and set the heat to low—cook for 15 minutes. Now you have pure essence of chicken and onion, an amazing amount of savory liquid. Add 3 cups water, 1 celery rib and some inner leaves, a carrot cut into chunks, a big pinch of dried thyme, 1 clove, 1 bay leaf, and 3 garlic cloves. Cover and simmer gently—don't let it boil—for 20 minutes. Strain and skim. To make a rich but elegant chicken soup, poach 2 chicken breasts in the microwave (page 48), dice them, and sauté briefly in melted butter before adding them to the soup, along with sliced scallions, sautéed mushrooms, ribbons of spinach, whatever you have on hand. Taste for seasoning and serve immediately. Serves 4.*

## Lentil Soup

This recipe isn't very different from most of the ones that appear on the lentil packages, except that it cooks for 2 hours, more than twice as long as ordinary lentil soups. The crucial ingredient is the ham bone, which adds a huge amount of flavor to this easy soup.

It's worth having a ham just to make this soup, but a ham hock works perfectly well too.

*Serves 6*

1 ham bone or ham hock

1 pound dried lentils, sorted
  and rinsed

2 quarts water

1 onion stuck with 2 cloves

1 celery rib and a few
  celery leaves

2 carrots

2 garlic cloves

1 bay leaf

salt and freshly ground pepper
  to taste

The Garnish:

croutons fried in olive oil with
  chopped garlic

sautéed slices of sausage

crumbled crisp-fried bacon

In a large heavy soup pot, combine everything but the salt, pepper, and garnishes and bring to a boil. Cover the pot tightly, reduce the heat, and simmer for 2 hours, stirring from time to time.

Remove the ham bone, vegetables, and bay leaf. When the ham bone is cool enough to remove the meat, chop it into bite-sized little bits.

You can puree the soup or not, as you like; we like it smooth. Using a hand blender, puree the soup right in the pot or pass it through a food mill. Taste for salt and pepper and adjust seasoning. Add the bits of ham to the soup.

Serve hot in warmed soup bowls with one of the garnishes. Be sure the croutons are piping hot, straight from the skillet—they should sizzle when they hit the soup.

*The soup freezes well. Leftover soup may thicken; you can thin it with a little cream or water.*

*We like all bean soups tweaked with a little jolt of vinegar just before serving.*

*Try adding 3 or 4 tablespoons chopped fresh ginger along with the onion for extra snap.*

*Speedy Onion Soup*

*Reminiscent of the legendary time-consuming French classic. Sauté 3 cups sliced onion in 4 tablespoons (½ stick) butter until golden. Add 6 10½-ounce cans of condensed beef broth (undiluted) and simmer for 20 minutes. Put 6 thick slices of toasted French bread into a deep casserole. Pour in the onions and broth and cover the top with ¾ cup each of grated Parmesan and Gruyère. Dot the top with 3 tablespoons cold butter bits and bake the soup in a 400° oven until the top is crusty and golden. Serves 6.*

↪ *Check the ham bone for any lingering cloves if they were used to decorate the ham—the cloves in the onion are plenty.*

↪ SPLIT PEA SOUP: *This is the very same soup, made with split peas instead of lentils.*

# Black Bean Soup

This is the classic soup that was served at the Coach House, a beloved New York restaurant owned by Leon Lianides. Mr. Lianides was generous with his recipes, which may be one reason they're classics—they appear in a number of standard cookbooks. This is an interesting soup that takes a long time to cook but not much actual work. It's flavored with both ham and beef, then finished with Madeira, chopped hard-cooked eggs, and paper-thin lemon slices. We've frankly never eaten a better bean soup, so we're offering it as the standard.

*Serves 12*

| | |
|---|---|
| 2 cups dried black beans, sorted and rinsed | 1 ham bone, including the rind, or 2 ham hocks |
| 4 tablespoons (½ stick) butter | 3 pounds beef or veal bones |
| 2 large onions, coarsely chopped | 8 peppercorns |
| 2 garlic cloves, crushed | 2 tablespoons flour |
| 3 leeks, thoroughly cleaned and coarsely chopped | 4 to 5 quarts water |
| 1 celery rib, coarsely chopped | ½ cup Madeira or sherry |
| 2 bay leaves | chopped parsley |
| 2 cloves | 2 finely chopped hard-cooked eggs |
| | 12 very thin lemon slices |

Soak the beans overnight in water to cover. The next day, melt the butter in a stockpot with the vegetables, bay leaves, and cloves; sauté over medium heat for 3 minutes. Add the ham bone and beef bones and cook for 3 to 4 minutes more, then add the peppercorns and flour and blend well. Cook for 2 to 3 minutes, then add the water and bring to a boil.

Reduce the heat, skim, and simmer covered, for about 8 hours.

Drain the soaked beans, add to the pot, and simmer, uncovered, for 2½ hours more, stirring occasionally. Add more water if it gets too thick or the beans are not completely covered.

Remove from the heat, discard the bones, cloves, and bay leaves, and puree the soup through a food mill—a hand blender will be overwhelmed by this job. Taste for seasoning, add the Madeira, and bring to a boil. Turn off the heat and serve immediately, garnished with the parsley, eggs, and one lemon slice for each bowl.

➤ *Make a quick version of the soup with two 16-ounce cans of black beans, a can of beef broth, and a little smoked meat: sautéed bacon, smoked beef sausage, or bits of ham. Add a couple of minced cloves of garlic and simmer the soup for 30 minutes. Puree it and finish with the Coach House signature of Madeira or sherry, hard-cooked eggs, and the thin slices of lemon.*

# U.S. Senate Bean Soup

The Senate dining room has a lot of famous dishes—rum pie, Senate salad (with ten ingredients from ten different states)—but this is the most famous, the dish that inspired a filibuster when its place on the menu was threatened.

*Serves 8*

1 pound dried navy beans, sorted
   and rinsed

3 quarts cold water

3 medium potatoes, cooked and
   mashed

6 celery ribs, finely chopped

¼ cup chopped parsley

2 medium onions, minced

1 large ham hock

salt and freshly ground pepper to taste

Soak the beans overnight in water to cover; drain. Cover the beans with fresh water in a heavy pot and cook, uncovered, over medium heat until tender, about 1 hour. Drain the beans and return them to the pot with 3 quarts water and the remaining ingredients. Season to taste and cook slowly, uncovered, for 2 hours, stirring occasionally to prevent scorching.

Remove the ham hock and take the meat off the bones when it's cool. Cut the meat into bite-sized pieces and add to the soup. In the Senate, the soup is served in individual earthenware bowls with garlic bread on the side.

# Cream of Mushroom Soup

hen stores carried only white button mushrooms, making a memorable cream of mushroom soup was hardly worth the chopping or wasting a stash of homemade chicken broth. Now there are not only fresh exotic mushrooms but the richly flavored dried ones that can be kept indefinitely on the pantry shelf, making mushroom soup both easier to make and far more intense. The more varied the mushrooms you choose, the more elegant and interesting the soup. After you've made it a couple of times, you'll enjoy trying the options, including leaving out the cream altogether and adding barley or wild rice.

*Serves 8*

2½ ounces mixed dried mushrooms,
   such as porcini, cèpes, chanterelles

1½ pounds mixed fresh mushrooms,
   cleaned and trimmed, such as
   cremini, portobellos, shiitakes

4 tablespoons (½ stick) butter

1 tablespoon fresh lemon juice

2 garlic cloves, minced

½ medium onion, minced

1 teaspoon dried thyme leaves or
   1 tablespoon fresh

salt and freshly ground pepper to taste

pinch of cayenne pepper

¼ cup ruby port

5 cups homemade or condensed
   canned (undiluted) beef broth

1 cup half-and-half

3 large egg yolks

minced parsley and chives for garnish

Soak the dried mushrooms in cold water overnight. Drain the mushrooms and squeeze the juice into the soaking bowl. Pour the liquid through a fine-mesh strainer and reserve. Mince the mushrooms and reserve. Chop the fresh mushrooms and sauté them in the butter in a skillet over medium-high heat in 2 batches until flecked with brown. Transfer to a bowl with a slotted spoon, toss them with the lemon juice, and set aside. In a 3-quart saucepan, sauté the garlic and onion, seasoning it with the thyme, salt, pepper, and cayenne. When the onion is translucent, add the port, scraping the bottom of the pan, and simmer a minute or two to burn off the alcohol. Add the broth, the reserved dried mushroom liquid, and all the mushrooms. Bring to a slow simmer and cook over low heat for 30 minutes. Add the half-and-half and heat. Whisk the egg yolks with a couple of spoonfuls of the hot soup. Add the yolks to the pot and stir and cook until the soup is smooth and slightly thickened. Serve with the parsley and chives on top.

    *In lieu of egg yolks, the soup can be thickened with a cooked potato put through a potato ricer, whisked into some of the beef broth, and added to the finished soup. You could also sprinkle instant flour into the pan after the port wine deglaze, whisking to thicken into a light roux. Heat 2 cups of the beef broth to stir into the mixture before adding the cold liquids.*

    *If you use the flour thickening, you could add a cup of yogurt instead of the cream and it won't separate. Do not, however, bring it to a boil.*

    *To make a heartier main-dish soup, add slices of cooked smoked sausage or small chicken meatballs seasoned with garlic and lemon zest.*

    *If you cannot find a good selection of dried mushrooms locally, write to N.W. Mushroom Co., Inc., PO Box 2997, La Grande, OR 97850.*

# Vichyssoise

French chef Louis Diat created this luscious chilled version of the classic hot cream of leek and potato soup at New York's Ritz-Carlton Hotel in 1917. Years later, for sentimental reasons, he named it for the town nearest his home village—not for the unpopular wartime seat of the Vichy government. Although the erroneous connection riled his French patriot colleagues, none of them succeeded in getting him to change the name.

*Serves 6*

3 medium boiling potatoes, diced
6 leeks, white part only, thoroughly
    cleaned and finely sliced
1 quart homemade (page 25) or
    canned chicken or vegetable broth

salt to taste
1¼ cups heavy cream
1 tablespoon snipped chives plus
    more for garnish

Simmer the potatoes and leeks in the broth until the potatoes are very soft. Add salt and cool the soup for 30 minutes. Puree the cool mixture in a food processor in small batches, being careful not to process more than 30 seconds, or the potato starch will turn the soup to glue. Pour the soup through a strainer. Stir in the heavy cream and chives. Refrigerate, covered, preferably in a glass jar. Serve garnished with a few more chives.

*If you have a hand blender, puree the soup right in the pot.*

*For a tangy, less rich soup, substitute buttermilk for the heavy cream and float thin slices of cucumber on top.*

*For an elegant company first course, float a thin slice of cooked potato carrying a demitasse spoonful of caviar and a sprinkling of chives on top.*

CLASSIC AMERICAN FOOD WITHOUT FUSS

# New England Clam Chowder

*M*anhattan clam chowder lovers may rip this page out and light the grill with it, but we prefer our clam chowder without tomatoes. It used to be possible to turn out a decent spontaneous clam chowder with canned clams, but for some inexplicable reason they seem to have lost all taste and tenderness. The imported whole baby clams are a tad better, but the best alternative to steaming and chopping cherrystones or steamers yourself is to query your seafood purveyor. We've found tubs of chopped clams nestled in among the fillets in the cold months.

*Serves 8*

¼ pound smoky slab bacon, diced

1½ cups minced onion

1 tablespoon fresh thyme leaves or
    1 teaspoon dried

1 large bay leaf

freshly ground black pepper

pinch of cayenne pepper

6 medium new potatoes, peeled
    and diced

3 cups clam juice, including the liquor
    from the clams

1 quart chopped clams

1 cup heavy cream

1 cup half-and-half

¼ cup minced parsley for garnish

Sauté the bacon with the onion, thyme, bay leaf, pepper, and cayenne in a skil-let over medium-high heat until the bacon is rendered and slightly crisp. Add the diced potatoes and clam juice and simmer until the potatoes are almost done, about 6 minutes. Add the clams and simmer for another 6 minutes. Add the cream and half-

and-half, bring slowly to a boil, reduce the heat, and simmer for 5 minutes. Serve in heated bowls with the parsley garnish.

> ✎ *It's easy to vary this chowder. Use salmon instead of clams and dill instead of thyme. Substitute chicken broth for clam juice and make corn chowder by creaming the corn with some of the half-and-half before adding it. Add a few strips of roasted red pepper and taste for salt.*

*Salads*

# Crab Louis

*W*hen Enrico Caruso sang with the Met in Seattle in 1904, he ate the kitchen out of the chef's sensational salad, Crab Louis. Succulent Dungeness crab is rarely found off the West Coast, but this old favorite is just as good with Maryland blue crab or the almost equally scarce Florida stone crab.

*Serves 4*

**The Sauce:**

1 cup mayonnaise, preferably
   Hellmann's
3 tablespoons chili sauce
½ cup sour cream
1 teaspoon Worcestershire sauce

dash of Tabasco sauce
2 tablespoons finely chopped scallion,
   including some of the green
¼ teaspoon salt
2 tablespoons minced parsley

**To Assemble the Salad:**

2 ripe Hass avocados, peeled and
   halved
2 tablespoons fresh lemon juice
salt and freshly ground pepper
2 heads of Bibb lettuce
1½ pounds lump or backfin crabmeat,
   well picked over

4 hard-cooked eggs, peeled and
   quartered
4 small ripe tomatoes, quartered and
   preferably peeled

Combine the sauce ingredients. Brush the avocado halves with lemon juice. Sprinkle with salt and pepper. Make a bed of lettuce on each serving plate and top with an avocado half, paring a thin slice off the bottom to make it stand upright. Reserve the slices for lids. Split the avocado lengthwise almost to the small end and spread slightly to hold the crab. Mask the crab with sauce and place the lid at an angle. Garnish with lightly salted egg and tomato wedges and pass any extra sauce at the table.

# Spinach Salad

This is the delicious main-dish salad served everywhere but particularly in California, the land of flat-leaf spinach and peerless luncheon salads, where it appears in many incarnations. For a refreshing side-dish salad, simply reduce the portions and omit the egg and bacon. It pairs very well with roast chicken or a thick grilled veal chop.

*Serves 4*

**The Dressing:**

1 tablespoon honey Dijon or hot-
  sweet mustard
1 garlic clove, smashed and minced
  (see page 112)
1 tablespoon minced fresh dill

1½ tablespoons fresh lemon juice
5 tablespoons mixture of extra-virgin
  olive oil and safflower oil
1 tablespoon heavy cream or light
  mayonnaise

**The Salad:**

2 hard-cooked eggs, peeled

3 pounds flat-leaf or baby spinach, stems removed

6 white mushrooms, stems removed and caps sliced

6 strips of bacon, fried crisp, drained, and crumbled

6 scallions (including 1 inch of green), halved lengthwise and slivered, or 6 thin slices red onion

1 cup garlic croutons

In a large mixing bowl, whisk the dressing ingredients together until creamy. Taste and adjust the seasoning if necessary. Press the egg yolks through a fine-mesh strainer and finely chop the whites, keeping them separate. Set aside. Add the spinach and mushrooms to the salad bowl and toss well to coat. Divide among 4 serving bowls. Sprinkle the egg white around the outside edge. In the center, sprinkle the bacon, scallions, and egg yolk. Top with croutons.

➤ *For a delicious small supper, coat warm cooked cheese ravioli in the dressing before tossing with the salad. Omit the egg and croutons, substituting grated Parmesan.*

➤ *Instead of the raw sliced mushrooms, add wedges of warm grilled portobello and thinly sliced ham or prosciutto cut into fine strips.*

➤ *Use drained yogurt to cream the dressing, omit the egg and croutons, and add crumbled feta cheese, minced dill, and toasted pine nuts.*

➤ *For a blue cheese version, make the dressing with mayonnaise thinned with a little white wine vinegar, lemon juice, and vegetable oil. Season it with a dash of Worcestershire sauce, minced scallions or chives, and crumbled blue cheese. Omit the mushrooms and egg.*

# Potato Salad

We know we're on thin ice here, recommending one kind of potato salad over another. Passions run high on this subject, and regional preferences are powerful. The potatoes can be baking potatoes (which give a raggedy-looking potato salad that's creamier) or new potatoes, which hold their shape. We like new potatoes with their skins on—less fuss and more flavor.

This is more or less the classic potato salad that appears on picnic tables throughout the Midwest and the South—see the notes for other options, which are indeed many. But once you get beyond potatoes, some kind of onion, mayonnaise, and salt and pepper, almost everything else is a question of taste.

*Serves 8*

2 pounds Red Bliss or other waxy
    new potatoes
½ cup sliced scallion, including some
    of the green, or 1 medium red
    onion, finely chopped
3 celery ribs, finely chopped, including
    some of the inner yellow leaves
½ green bell pepper, finely chopped
¼ cup chopped parsley
salt and freshly ground pepper to taste

1 to 3 teaspoons dry mustard,
    preferably Colman's, to taste
2 tablespoons cider vinegar or to taste
1½ to 2 cups mayonnaise, preferably
    Hellmann's (or half mayonnaise
    and half sour cream), as needed
3 hard-cooked eggs, peeled and
    chopped
2 teaspoons celery seeds
paprika for garnish

Wash the potatoes gently but thoroughly. Arrange them in a steaming basket inside a large pot. Steam them, covered, over an inch or two of boiling water for 15 to 20 minutes or until they're just tender; drain them well.

While the potatoes are still hot, cut them into rough chunks about an inch square. Put them in a bowl and toss with the vegetables and salt and pepper, starting with 1½ teaspoons salt.

In a separate bowl, mix the mustard with the vinegar until perfectly smooth, then mix in the mayonnaise. Mix the dressing into the potatoes, trying not to crush them. Scatter the celery seeds and eggs over all, mix again, and sprinkle the top of the salad with paprika. Cover the salad and set aside to chill for at least 2 hours.

🍃 *Be sure your potatoes are the same size so they'll cook evenly.*

🍃 *Speed up the prep by cutting potatoes into ⅓-inch dice; steam them or cook them in the microwave (7 to 10 minutes).*

🍃 *Some options to add to taste: pickle relish, snipped dill, snipped chives, grated horseradish or Dijon mustard in the mayonnaise.*

🍃 *To improve the taste of commercial mayonnaise: Whisk an egg yolk and a little fresh lemon juice in a bowl and add the mayonnaise ¼ cup at a time, whisking thoroughly until you have a smooth sauce.*

🍃 The Classic Cooked Dressing: *Your grandmother probably made potato salad with a cooked dressing that has a sweet and sour tang. This isn't hard: Just mix in a double boiler 6 tablespoons flour, 6 tablespoons sugar, 3 large eggs, beaten, ¾ teaspoon salt, ½ cup cider vinegar, 1 teaspoon dry mustard, and 1½ cups water. Cook over medium heat, stirring frequently, until creamy. If you need more flour, add it—just be sure to cook the dressing long enough to cook the extra flour. The dressing will keep in the refrigerator for a week. Toss it with hot potatoes, then add celery, minced onion, chopped hard-cooked eggs, celery seed, and salt and pepper to taste.*

🍃 *Give the hot potatoes a head start on flavor by tossing them with ¼ cup fresh lemon juice mixed with ¼ cup safflower oil and salt and pepper to taste. Then you can cut the mayonnaise to 1 cup.*

≈ FRENCH POTATO SALAD: *Toss the hot potato cubes with a splash of white wine, then a lemon vinaigrette (3 parts olive oil to 1 part lemon juice—a little grated lemon zest and/or minced garlic won't hurt). Add snipped chives and parsley (even a little mint if you like) with salt and pepper to taste. Serve warm.*

≈ HOT GERMAN POTATO SALAD: *While the potatoes are cooking, fry 1 strip of bacon per person until crisp; set aside, reserving the bacon fat. Add some minced garlic and chopped shallot to the hot bacon fat and cook briefly. Add 1 tablespoon wine vinegar per person to the skillet and keep warm. Toss the hot cooked potato cubes with olive oil. Add the hot seasoned bacon fat to the potatoes and toss well. Add salt and pepper to taste, chopped chives or scallions, and a good handful of chopped parsley. Serve hot, with the reserved bacon crumbled over the top.*

# Coleslaw

Here's another simple American dish with a number of classic preparations, all passionately defended by one group or another. Around Memphis the coleslaw has ballpark mustard in it; in the South it's either slathered with mayonnaise—as served in the Mayonnaise Belt—or made simply with oil, vinegar, and sugar. We like the Midwestern version, made in moments and made ahead.

Coleslaw is always refreshing and seems to go with almost everything, from ham to barbecue to fried chicken. And besides, even with mayonnaise, it's incredibly good for you.

*Serves 6*

1 small head of green cabbage
   (not savoy)
½ cup mayonnaise, preferably
   Hellmann's or Best Foods

½ cup sour cream
cider vinegar to taste
Dijon mustard to taste
salt and freshly ground pepper to taste

Core the cabbage, remove the outer leaves, and cut into wedges for slicing or grating. The grating disk of a food processor works very well for hurry-up slaw, but superthin slices look better and have better texture. Mix the mayonnaise and sour cream until perfectly smooth, then add vinegar to taste—start with a couple of tablespoons—and Dijon mustard (start with a teaspoon). Add salt and pepper and let the coleslaw season for several hours. Drain if necessary just before serving.

➢ *Try using half red cabbage (in winter the leaves are a little tougher), half green. Grate in a carrot or a little green bell pepper, a little onion or some radishes, or some apple. Snipped dill is a delicious option. Celery seed is as good in coleslaw as it is in potato salad. If the cider vinegar isn't giving you enough of the sweet-sour balance, you may need to add a little sugar.*

➢ *Using yogurt for part of the dressing seems like a good idea, but it doesn't really have the right chemistry for cabbage. If you want a lower-fat dressing, use buttermilk for some of the mayonnaise and add a little grated lemon zest.*

➢ *James Beard has a wonderful red cabbage coleslaw using more sour cream than mayonnaise, sliced scallions, a little snipped dill, and capers.*

➢ *If you're making a red cabbage slaw in winter and the cabbage is a little too chewy, blanch the cabbage first by dropping it into a pot of boiling water for a couple of minutes—drain well, let it cool, and proceed with the recipe.*

➢ *If you want a little creaminess but not a lot of mayonnaise, just add a spoonful to a classic vinaigrette made with cider vinegar.*

# Greek Salad

*A* really well-made Greek salad is a revelation, at least compared to the uninspired Greek salads that turn up in most ethnic restaurants and diners. This one works as a side salad or even as the main course, served with some good rustic bread or warm pita bread.

*Serves 4*

4 or 5 large tomatoes, cut into chunks

1 cucumber, peeled and cut into
    chunks

3 green bell peppers, cut into chunks

1 bunch of scallions (both white and
    firm green parts), chopped, or
    ½ cup chopped sweet onion

½ pound imported feta cheese,
    crumbled

¼ cup chopped parsley

2 teaspoons salt

1 tablespoon red wine vinegar or fresh
    lemon juice

¼ cup extra-virgin olive oil

¼ teaspoon dried oregano or to taste

romaine leaves

16 Kalamata olives

In a large bowl, mix the tomatoes, cucumber, peppers, scallions, feta, and parsley. In a small bowl, mix the salt and vinegar together until the salt dissolves, then add the oil. Pour the dressing over the salad and sprinkle with oregano; mix the dressing into the salad well. Line a large platter with romaine leaves and arrange the salad on top. Strew olives over the salad and serve.

*In some versions, there are anchovy fillets on top of the salad, about 2 for each person. Flaked tuna is another option to make this more of a main dish.*

# Salade Niçoise

How exactly to make the classic Niçoise salad is a hotly contested subject in Nice, where the ex-mayor, the reigning culinary authority, has announced the real thing has nothing cooked in it: only lettuce, tomato, tuna, and anchovies. That would mean no potatoes, no hard-cooked eggs, and no green beans, elements Americans have come to love in this wonderful salad. But the mayor has since been imprisoned for corruption, so we take his edict with a little *sel*.

The crucial thing is to use only imported tuna packed in extra-virgin olive oil, which delivers astounding flavor compared to our lunch-box tuna. Genova is a good brand that's widely available in little gold cans.

You can serve the salad several ways: composed on a giant platter from which people help themselves, composed on individual plates, or tossed in a big salad bowl. For the tossed salad, tear the lettuce leaves into bite-sized pieces; for the composed salads, they're the bed for everything else.

*Serves 4*

**The Vinaigrette:**

2 tablespoons fresh lemon juice

2 tablespoons red wine vinegar

1 garlic clove, minced

1 teaspoon Dijon mustard

2 tablespoons chopped fresh
    herbs such as parsley, chives,
    and basil

salt and freshly ground pepper
    to taste

⅔ cup olive oil

**The Salad:**

4 medium new potatoes, scrubbed
  and diced (optional)

1 head of Boston lettuce, leaves
  separated

4 or 5 tomatoes, quartered, salted,
  and drained

½ pound green beans, steamed until
  crisp-tender

1 small cucumber, preferably Kirby,
  thinly sliced

1 green bell pepper, thinly sliced

2 hard-cooked eggs, peeled and
  quartered (optional)

2 6½-ounce cans Italian tuna packed
  in olive oil, drained

2 canned anchovy fillets, rinsed and
  chopped

Whisk the dressing ingredients together and set aside. You can make it earlier in the day.

Steam the potatoes until tender and toss them with a little of the vinaigrette. Arrange composed salads on the lettuce leaves, making little mounds of each element with cut vegetables placed decoratively around them. Pour the vinaigrette over the top. Or toss everything together with the vinaigrette in a large serving bowl.

*Other options: Add some Niçoise olives or capers.*

*In Nice, according to Riviera cuisine expert Colman Andrews, they salt the tomatoes 3 times: first when they're cut, again after they're drained, and a third time when they go into the salad. Worth a try.*

# Cobb Salad

*N*ot too many classic dishes come out of Hollywood, but this is one of them, named for Robert Cobb, the owner of the Brown Derby restaurant where it was born. At the restaurant a great production was made of it: The greens were chopped exuberantly with a knife and fork in front of the diner, then the rest was added with high drama. This is a great salad, served dramatically or not. The key is to chop everything into bite-sized pieces.

*Serves 4*

1 head of iceberg lettuce, chopped

12 leaves of romaine, chopped

1 bunch of watercress, chopped

4 celery ribs, sliced (optional)

1 avocado, cubed

2 large tomatoes, chopped

1 whole chicken breast, cooked, skin
   and bones removed, and meat
   chopped, about 1½ cups

2 hard-cooked eggs, peeled and
   chopped

¼ pound blue cheese, crumbled

12 strips of bacon, fried crisp, drained,
   and crumbled

6 tablespoons olive oil

2 tablespoons tarragon or white wine
   vinegar

salt and pepper to taste

1 garlic clove, smashed (see
   page 112)

Mix everything together in a big salad bowl except the last 7 ingredients. Scatter the eggs, cheese, and bacon over the salad. Mix the oil, vinegar, salt, pepper, and garlic in a screw-top jar and shake well. Strain the vinaigrette (or simply remove the garlic clove), then drizzle the vinaigrette over all, and toss at the table before serving.

*✐  Another option: Dress the salad greens and arrange them on individual plates. Add strips of chicken, bacon, eggs, tomato, avocado, and cheese on top.*

# Chicken Salad

Although it's hopelessly mired in jokes about ladies' luncheons, a really well-made chicken salad is just great—perfect on a hot day when you're hungry but don't want anything oppressive. It can be as simple as chicken bites covered with mayonnaise thinned with lemon juice—add chopped celery and salt and pepper.

Lots of cooks think the tastiest chicken is roasted, but you can also poach the chicken on top of the stove or in the microwave, which will give you a better texture. Take-out roast chicken is fine, of course. If you're making chicken soup, it's worth dropping a few chicken breasts in during the last half hour of cooking so you can make this salad.

It seems that chicken salad should improve if made ahead so that the flavors develop, but we like it best made just before serving, and it's so easy that a little last-minute work doesn't present a problem.

*Serves 6*

**The Chicken:**

3 whole chicken breasts

salt and freshly ground pepper to taste

**The Dressing:**

3 tablespoons fresh lemon juice

½ cup mayonnaise, preferably Hellmann's or Best Foods

½ cup sour cream

salt and freshly ground pepper to taste

**To Assemble the Salad:**

¼ cup finely chopped scallion,
  including some of the green

¼ cup finely chopped celery, including
  some of the inner leaves

¼ cup finely chopped fresh parsley

1 tablespoon chopped fresh tarragon
  or dill (optional)

grated zest of 1 lemon (optional)

¼ cup sliced almonds, toasted
  (optional)

1 tablespoon drained capers
  (optional)

Preheat the oven to 500°. Place the chicken breasts on a baking sheet and salt and pepper them all over. Roast for 10 minutes on each side, a total of 20 minutes. Check for doneness; the juices should run clear. When the chicken is cool, remove skin and bones and pull or chop into large pieces.

To make the dressing, in a small bowl, mix the lemon juice with the mayonnaise until smooth. Whisk in the sour cream until smooth. Add salt and pepper.

Put the chicken and all the other salad ingredients into a large bowl and mix well. Add the dressing and mix thoroughly.

➤ *If you want to include dark meat, use chicken thighs, which will take another 10 to 15 minutes in the oven.*

➤ *To poach the chicken in the microwave, put the breast halves in 1 cup of canned chicken broth, cover, and cook on HIGH for 6 minutes.*

➤ *To poach on top of the stove, bring 4 cups of water to a boil, drop in the chicken, and simmer uncovered for 15 minutes. Cover, turn off the heat, and let steep for 30 minutes.*

➤ CURRIED DRESSING: *Use lime juice instead of lemon and add a little apple cider to the dressing along with a teaspoon (or more to taste) of very mild sweet curry powder or garam masala and a jot of honey. Don't use dill or tarragon. Add some cubed fruit and nuts: melon, apricots, apples, dried currants, toasted almonds or cashews. Serve a spoonful of chutney on the side.*

# Caesar Salad

This king of all salads is named not after Julius Caesar but after the brother of its inventor, Alex Cardini, whose brother Caesar, a Tijuana restaurateur, devised the dressing. The salad was created to honor the pilots of Rockwell Field Air Base in San Diego, and its original name was Aviator's Salad (Alex had been an ace pilot in World War I). We've made the dressing simpler by blending it all together, so you can prepare it ahead.

Caesar salad can be either a main course for a light meal or a first course. The main rule to follow is to have very crisp greens.

*Serves 4*

**The Dressing:**

1 large egg at room temperature, dunked into boiling water for 1 minute

1 garlic clove, pressed or minced

1 tablespoon fresh lime or lemon juice

1 teaspoon Worcestershire sauce

1 teaspoon anchovy paste

¼ cup extra-virgin olive oil

salt and freshly ground pepper to taste

**The Salad:**

1 large head of romaine lettuce, torn into bite-sized pieces

1 cup garlic croutons

¼ cup grated Parmesan cheese

In a screw-top jar, mix together the dressing ingredients, shake vigorously to blend, and taste for seasoning.

Put the greens in the serving bowl and toss with a little salt. Shake the dressing again, strain, and pour the dressing over the salad. Scatter the croutons over the salad and sprinkle on the cheese. Toss at the table and serve.

➣ *It makes a difference, subtle but distinctive, if you grate the Parmesan in a hand-held drum grater—it has a fluffy texture, as opposed to the little shards you get with an ordinary box grater.*

➣ *You can use 2 mashed anchovy fillets instead of the anchovy paste if you'd rather.*

➣ *If you're making the dressing more than a few hours ahead, strain and refrigerate it to keep the garlic from overpowering it. Bring to room temperature before serving.*

# Main Dishes

# Beef Stroganoff

This imperial Russian classic has been pitifully maltreated since it hit the American gourmet scene in the late forties. Then it was de rigueur for impressing the boss; unfortunately, it usually languished in curdled discomfort in a silver chafing dish. Stroganoff is one of those dishes that "when it was good it was very, very good—and when it was bad it was horrid." James McNair's updated recipe in his *Beef Cookbook* should help return stroganoff to its royal glory. Look for tenderloin tips—the flat end of the whole tenderloin—to help offset the cost of the wild mushrooms. This is clearly a special-occasion dish.

*Serves 6*

6 quarts water

salt to taste

1 pound wide egg noodles

1½ pounds beef tenderloin, well
    trimmed

1½ cups homemade or condensed
    canned (undiluted) beef broth

¼ pound (1 stick) unsalted butter

1½ tablespoons flour

1 cup sour cream

1 pound fresh wild mushrooms, such
    as chanterelles, morels, porcini,
    or shiitakes, sliced

freshly ground black pepper to taste

¼ cup minced shallot

3 tablespoons dry sherry, or to taste

fresh thyme leaves or minced parsley
    for garnish

Bring the water to a boil for the egg noodles and add salt. Meanwhile, slice the beef across the grain into ¼ by 2-inch strips. Set aside. In a 2-cup glass measure, bring the broth to a simmer in the microwave. Meanwhile, melt 3 tablespoons of the butter in a saucepan over medium-high heat and whisk in the flour and some salt, continuing to stir for a couple of minutes. Add the simmering broth all at once and whisk until smooth and thick. Remove from the heat and stir in the sour cream. Set aside.

In a skillet, sauté the mushrooms in another 3 tablespoons of the butter over medium-high heat, shaking the pan and tossing them around until they take on some color, about 4 minutes. Salt and pepper, remove from the skillet, and set aside. (Keep the skillet on the stove to cook the beef.)

At this point, cook the noodles in the rapidly boiling water until just tender. Using a long handled strainer, scoop the noodles from the water and put them in a bowl. Stir in a little soft butter to keep the noodles from sticking together and keep them warm over half of the boiling water.

In the mushroom skillet, melt the remaining butter and quickly sauté the shallot and beef, again shaking the pan and tossing the strips until the beef is golden brown, about 3 minutes. Add the sherry, let it sizzle briefly, and add the mushrooms and sauce, reheating over low heat for a couple of minutes. Serve the stroganoff over the buttered noodles and garnish with the thyme or parsley.

## New England Boiled Dinner

New England boiled dinner bespeaks salt-cured corned beef, which is seldom found outside the region. Of course you can corn your own, but that task isn't on *our* to-do list. Regular corned beef, if you can find one that isn't too lean to be cooked to juicy tenderness, is the common substitute. Fresh brisket is another tasty alternative that is readily available, inexpensive, and well suited to a long gentle simmer in nothing more exotic than plain water. Once tender, it's ready to be accompanied by either the classic vegetables or your own favorites. Since the cooked meat can rest in the refrigerator for several days without harm, the complete dinner can be assembled whenever you're ready. Beware: Thinly sliced brisket makes splendid sandwiches for midnight snitches.

*Serves 4*

1 3½-pound second-cut corned beef or fresh brisket

2 bay leaves

2 teaspoons black peppercorns

2 cloves

4 small white onions

4 medium carrots

4 parsnips

4 medium new potatoes

4 small white turnips

½ head of green cabbage, cut into 4 wedges

4 medium beets, trimmed and scrubbed

Rinse the brisket in cool running water and put it in a heavy lidded kettle or dutch oven. Don't trim the fat. Pour in enough water to cover by ½ inch. Add the bay leaves, peppercorns, and cloves and bring the water to a boil. Reduce the heat and keep it at a very gentle simmer. A Flame-Tamer under the kettle will prevent bubble-overs. Cook the meat for 2 to 2½ hours or until the tip of a sharp knife pierces it easily. Add all the vegetables except the cabbage and beets during the last 20 minutes of cooking. Then add the cabbage for another 15 minutes. Meanwhile, steam the beets in the microwave in ½ cup of water for about 22 minutes on high, or cook them in boiling salted water until tender. When the beets are cool enough to handle, slip off the skins and keep the beets warm or reheat if necessary.

Trim any clinging fat from the brisket, slice it thinly, and lay the slices out in the center of a heated platter. Surround the meat with the vegetables and serve with a grainy mustard or grated horseradish or combine the two—or try prepared horseradish mixed with sour cream.

➤ *Today's lean briskets can be dry. Keep testing for doneness so the meat doesn't overcook.*

➤ *If you're using fresh brisket instead of corned beef, you can creatively season the simmering water without fear of dishonoring the classic recipe. Try covering the meat with a couple of bottles of North Carolina's Blenheim ginger ale. The superzingy version with a bright red cap imparts a wonderful piquant edge to the meat's beefy flavor. If you can't find Blenheim in a local* store, you can mail-order it by phoning (800) 270-9344. Or, use a Jamaican ginger beer.

☞ If you have enough leftovers for sandwiches, slice the meat paper-thin, pile it on buttered potato bread toast, and dress the sandwich with plenty of Dijon mayonnaise or zesty creamed horseradish sauce. Pick up a jar of Mrs. Fanning's Bread & Butter Pickles and make a basket of hot Saratoga chips (page 132). Along with little crocks of tomato soup, this will make a dandy supper.

☞ You can also dress up the homely brisket by glazing it in a 375° oven after it's been simmered. Stud the meat with whole cloves and drizzle it with maple syrup spiked with a dash of Tabasco sauce. Serve with roasted Idaho potato halves brushed with garlic butter and thyme. Yet another way to serve a brisket is to douse it with a bottle of smoky barbecue sauce and charcoal-grill it.

# Yankee Pot Roast

*J*ames Beard said that no one really knows the origin of this dish or what precise ingredients go into it—still, we've been eating it at diners for years and loving it, and we know what we mean when we say we'd like to have a good Yankee pot roast for dinner. Basically it's just a good chunk of beef braised with a minimum of herbs and spices and garnished with lots of root vegetables—especially rutabaga, the Yankee element—and served with gravy. Like all pot roasts, this one will be even better the next day, if you can wait that long.

*Serves 6*

1 4-pound boneless chuck roast, tied
salt and freshly ground pepper to taste
flour for dredging
2 tablespoons vegetable oil
1 cup homemade or canned beef
    broth
1½ teaspoons dried thyme or leaves
    from 4 fresh sprigs
1 onion stuck with 1 clove
2 bay leaves

8 small carrots, whole, or 4 large
    ones, cut into chunks
3 potatoes, peeled and quartered
1 small rutabaga, cut into 1-inch
    cubes
2 turnips, peeled and cut into 1-inch
    chunks
2 celery ribs, cut into chunks
instant flour, such as Wondra, for
    thickening gravy

Preheat the oven to 350°.

Pat the roast dry with paper towels and rub it all over with salt and pepper, then with flour. Heat the oil in a dutch oven with a tight-fitting cover over medium-high heat. When it's hot, put the roast in to brown, being careful not to pierce the meat—use tongs to move it around. Brown the meat well on all sides, then add ½ cup of the broth and the thyme, onion, and bay leaves.

Cover the pot tightly, using a layer of foil if it doesn't fit closely, and put the pot roast in the oven. After an hour, carefully turn the meat over. Cook for another 30 minutes, then add the carrots, potatoes, rutabaga, turnips, and celery. Stir them into the liquid, removing the roast momentarily if necessary, so that the vegetables are bathed in the sauce. Sprinkle a little salt and pepper over the vegetables and cover the pot. Return to the oven for 45 minutes or until the meat and vegetables are done.

Transfer the roast to a platter and cover with foil to keep warm. Either arrange the vegetables around the meat or pile them into their own serving bowl. Remove the bay leaves.

To make the gravy, remove all but a tablespoon or two of fat from the dutch oven—the easiest way is to pour the drippings into a fat-separating pitcher. Return the drippings to the dutch oven and add the remaining beef broth, stirring well to pick up all the little bits at the bottom of the pot. Add the instant flour as needed to thicken the gravy, then cook it over medium-low heat for 3 minutes.

Remove the strings from the roast and cut it into thick slices to serve.

*The root vegetables give the gravy a sweet taste. You may want to correct that with a dash of Worcestershire sauce or a splash of strong coffee. If you have some demi-glace (concentrated meat stock) lurking in your refrigerator (which is a good idea; D'Artagnan makes a good one that's kept in the refrigerated case of specialty stores and can be ordered by mail at [800] 327-8246), by all means add a spoonful or two to the gravy.*

*It's not classic, but 6 chopped garlic cloves thrown into the pot as it goes into the oven are delicious. A big splash of red wine doesn't hurt, either.*

*If you want even more vegetables, try parsnips, in chunks, and chunks of celery root. A cup of frozen pearl onions is nice, too.*

# Meat Loaf

There must be people who don't like meat loaf, but we've never met them. And we've hardly ever met a meat loaf we didn't like. This homiest of all dishes is best when it's simplest—which is rare; everything from oatmeal to soy sauce gets tucked into meat loaf, and you may want to try your hand at playing with this dish too.

But before you get creative, try making this simple recipe once, just to get your bearings and think about what other tastes might work here.

Put the loaf together as early in the day as you can. Leftover meat loaf tastes better because the flavors have had a chance to marry, and you can get a head start on that process by mixing the loaf together up to 8 hours before baking it. If you don't have time early in the day, even an hour or two will make a difference.

*Serves 8*

3 pounds meat loaf mix: veal, pork,
   and beef

2 tablespoons butter

1 large onion, minced

½ large green bell pepper, minced

2 garlic cloves, minced

2 tablespoons cream (optional)

1 scant teaspoon dried thyme or
   marjoram leaves

2 large eggs, lightly beaten

¼ cup fresh bread crumbs

1 teaspoon salt

1 teaspoon freshly ground pepper

¼ cup ketchup plus more to
   paint loaf

4 strips of bacon, preferably
   hardwood-smoked

Let the meat come to room temperature in a large bowl. Meanwhile, melt the butter in a small skillet over medium heat and add the onion, green pepper, and garlic; cook gently for about 3 minutes, stirring frequently, until soft. Add the remaining ingredients except bacon and mix very lightly but thoroughly with your hands. When it begins to come together, pick it up in one piece and move it to a pie plate or

shallow ovenproof dish. Mold it into a loaf shape and smear it with ketchup. Arrange the bacon strips over the top. Cover with plastic wrap and let rest in the refrigerator until 30 minutes before baking.

To bake, preheat the oven to 350°. Bake the meat loaf for 1 hour and 15 minutes or until a meat thermometer registers 140°. Remove it from the oven and let it rest for 10 minutes before serving.

    *The perfect companion is mashed or scalloped potatoes, with some sturdy greens like kale on the side.*

    *If you have a problem with air pockets in meat loaf, give the pan a spank on the counter before it goes into the oven.*

## Minimalist Pot Roast

Professional cooks know that there are only a handful of recipes from a given cookbook worth making more than once. We hope that's not true for this book, but this pot roast should surely be one of them.

It comes from Helen Witty, a prize-winning food magazine editor and writer with a practical eye on the home cook's needs. It's hard to believe that a recipe that includes just meat and an onion (okay, plus salt and pepper) could deliver so much flavor, but that it does. A good flavorful piece of meat is the key.

*Serves 6*

## Frittatas

*The versatile frittata is simply a flat omelet with chunky fillings bound by the cooked eggs encasing them. They're less fussy to make than rolled or country omelets because they can be prepared ahead, served at room temperature (though not refrigerated), and one 10-inch frittata serves 6 to 8. The best version is the familiar Spanish tortilla made with chopped onion, minced garlic, parsley, and thin slices of precooked new potatoes. In a nonstick skillet, sauté the onion and garlic in 3 tablespoons of olive oil until soft and add your choice of fresh herbs. Salt and pepper. Add 3 sliced cooked new potatoes and pour in 5 beaten eggs. Let the mixture set on the bottom over medium heat and finish the runny top quickly under a broiler or set the pan in a preheated 375° oven for 2 or 3 minutes. Slice into wedges and serve hot, warm, or at room temperature. Note: Frittatas can be baked with only egg whites, which set well and look surprisingly appetizing. Frittatas are delicious with added cheese and vegetables. Try sautéed slices of zucchini with basil and fontina, garlicky stir-fried spinach and grated Parmesan, roasted red peppers and provolone, or fold in a chunky Mexican salsa with diced Monterey Jack.*

1 4-pound boneless rump or chuck pot roast

salt and freshly ground pepper to taste

1 to 2 tablespoons beef fat, bacon fat, or oil

1 large onion, peeled and cut in half

1 cup homemade or canned beef broth

1 tablespoon instant flour, such as Wondra

Preheat the oven to 300°. Wipe the roast dry; salt and pepper it all over. Heat the fat in a dutch oven or other heavy pot with a tight-fitting lid until it's very hot, almost smoking. Sear the roast on all sides, turning often until it's lightly browned all over. Add the onion halves, cut side down. Cover the pot and set it in the oven.

Bake for about 3 hours or roughly 45 minutes per pound. Check after 2½ hours; the roast is done when a fork pierces it easily. Transfer the roast to a serving platter and keep it warm under a foil tent. Meanwhile, transfer the onion pieces to the platter and skim the fat from the juices, leaving just a tablespoon or two.

To make the gravy, return the juices to the pot and add the beef broth. Bring to a simmer. Sprinkle the surface with instant flour and whisk the gravy over medium heat until it's thickened to your taste. Check for seasoning.

*No one's stopping you from adding garlic cloves or thyme or carrots and potatoes during the last hour of cooking.*

*Leftovers make great roast beef hash (page 65). And you'll have lots of gravy, so be sure to serve the roast with mashed potatoes.*

# Steak au Poivre

Almost fifty years ago, French pepper steak became all the rage on the chic Continental restaurant scene, where it was often flamboyantly prepared tableside—flames leaping and scorched pepper fumes wafting over the tufted red velvet banquettes. Theatrics aside, Americans declared this dish their own; a good chunk of beef seems much more our style than prissy *escalopes de veau*. Fortunately, the best dishes always survive food fashion trends, and steak au poivre is one of them. It's utterly simple and delicious.

*Serves 4*

4 strip or rib eye steaks, 1¼ inches
 thick and well marbled
2½ tablespoons olive oil or roasted
 garlic oil
¼ cup black peppercorns or mixed
 colors

½ cup cognac or brandy
1 cup homemade or condensed
 canned (undiluted) beef broth
2 tablespoons cold butter
minced parsley for garnish

Blot the steaks dry with a paper towel. Rub all surfaces with the olive oil. Crack the peppercorns evenly in a spice mill or a mortar and pestle, leaving no large hard bits to startle diners. Rub the pepper into the oiled steaks on all sides and, if possible, store them overnight in the refrigerator, lightly covered with wax paper. Bring the meat to room temperature before panfrying in a heavy skillet—lined copper or cast iron.

Sear the steaks over medium-high heat for about 5 seconds on each side and, holding them with tongs, seal the edges as well. Turn the heat down to medium to cook the meat to your taste or about 4 minutes on each side for medium. (Heat that's too high will burn the pepper coating, which tastes nasty.) When the meat is cooked, transfer it to a heated platter. Pour the cognac in the hot pan, scraping the bottom and evaporating the alcohol rapidly. Add the broth and quickly reduce the mixture by a third. Holding the pan up over the heat, add the cold butter in chunks and swirl it into the liquid until it's melted and slightly thickened. Pour the sauce over the steaks and sprinkle with the minced parsley. Serve immediately with either crisp toast points or creamy garlic mashed potatoes to capture the sauce.

*The "21" Club in New York serves bourbon pepper steak made with ¼ cup Kentucky bourbon, ½ cup red wine, and ½ cup beef broth.*

*The steaks should be at least 1 inch thick. The pepper coating is too sharp for thin steaks.*

*Look for interesting peppercorns to mix together. A combination of black, white, and pink is best, although plain black Tellicherry or other pungent peppercorns will do the job well. You can also use already cracked black pepper to save a step.*

*You can use tenderloin instead of strip steaks, but the intensity of the coating seems to suit the heavier cuts better. Either way, buy prime or choice beef from a good butcher. With luck, it might even have a little age.*

*Heavy cream is often used in lieu of butter, but we prefer the French way.*

*This is an excellent recipe for charcoal cooking and a great way to dress up the ubiquitous grilled steak. The sauce can be made in the kitchen beforehand using a small rendered piece of fat trimmed from the steak as the flavor base. Bring the skillet out to the grill, heat it, and flip the cooked steaks into the sauce, drizzling the rest on top. If you're sensitive to pepper fumes—inevitable in the kitchen—outdoor grilling is the answer.*

# Deviled Short Ribs

*S*hort ribs seem to be more popular in the West, particularly Texas, where they are often added to a barbecue menu. When you remember that beef short ribs are removed from the bottom of the rib section, you'll realize why the meat is so tasty and succulent. We think roast beef bones and the meat between them make the tastiest chewing around. Since short ribs *look* rather unappetizing, you might pass them by as overpriced tough old stew bones, forgetting that they're truly a beef delicacy.

*Serves 4*

**The Sauce:**

1 onion, chopped

6 garlic cloves, smashed and peeled
   (see page 112)

2 tablespoons Dijon mustard

1 tablespoon chili powder

2 teaspoons salt

1 teaspoon cayenne pepper

2 teaspoons sugar

1 cup dry red wine

**The Ribs:**

4 to 5 pounds (2 to 3 pieces per
   person) beef short ribs

flour for dusting

salt and freshly ground pepper to taste

Preheat the oven to 425°. Mince all the sauce ingredients, except the wine, in a food processor. Add the wine and blend. Or mince the onion and garlic and shake all the ingredients in a screw-top jar to blend. Dust the ribs lightly with flour, salt, and pepper, shaking off the excess. Roast the ribs, uncovered, in a large skillet or roaster with a lid until they're browned handsomely, about 30 minutes. Reduce the heat to 325°, add the sauce, cover the pan, and bake for 1½ hours. Or marinate the ribs in the sauce for 1 hour and cook over low embers on a charcoal grill for 30 to 45 minutes, turning and basting often. Serve with hash browns (page 134).

# Roast Beef Hash

The price of a standing rib roast shouldn't be uttered in the same breath as "hash," never mind "leftovers." We can't imagine savoring the rare remains better than by thinly slicing them onto bakery pumpernickel, spread with Inglehoffer's zesty cream horseradish. However, in case you're stuck with the outside cut, the tender but well-done meat that surrounds the top of the roast, and the sweet tidbits between the ribs, think hash and consider some of the other interesting options at the end of the recipe.

*Serves 4*

4 medium russet potatoes, peeled

1¼ cups homemade or condensed canned (undiluted) beef broth

3 tablespoons vegetable oil

1 cup finely chopped onion

3 garlic cloves, chopped

½ teaspoon dried rosemary, crushed

½ teaspoon dried thyme leaves

3 cups chopped leftover roast beef

salt and freshly ground pepper to taste

Tabasco sauce to taste

Steam the potatoes in the microwave in a small amount of beef broth for about 6 minutes or until the tip of a knife slides easily into the middle. Cool them just enough to dice and let them sit in beef broth to soak up some flavor. Heat the oil in a skillet over medium-high heat and add the onion, garlic, and herbs, stirring until the garlic is softened. Add the potatoes and toss them until they start to turn golden. Add the meat, salt and pepper, and Tabasco. If the hash seems dry, moisten it with more beef broth.

➤ *Adding either Worcestershire or A.1. sauce would be appropriate.*

➤ *For a deliciously irreverent touch, moisten the hash with Chinese oyster sauce.*

✒ *Try making "fresh" hash by frying chopped raw salmon steak in the same manner (use chicken broth instead of beef broth) and seasoning it with minced dill, snipped chives, and a little heavy cream spiked with mustard.*

✒ *Red flannel hash is made with leftover corned beef from a New England boiled dinner (page 53); add diced lean salt pork, boiled beets, and a splash or two of heavy cream.*

✒ *Leftover turkey and stuffing makes a great hash—particularly if you saved some gravy to moisten it with.*

✒ *Try leftover roast chicken and corn bread, sweet potato, onion, cilantro, and smoky chipotle sauce.*

# Beef Stew

Not only every cook but every cook in every country has a pet recipe for stew. Not surprising since the humble stew never climbed the social ladder or made it to the altar of haute cuisine but survived as an easy, frugal dish to nourish families. The original American prairie stew was often a rib-sticking mess of no-name meat and potatoes slogging around in murky gravy. Things improved immensely when the stew pot dipped deeply from the melting pot and more refined variations kicked in. It was then that the romance and ritual of this simple braise pushed beef stew right up there with meat loaf in the annals of American comfort food. It can be served with the usual vegetables, just with mashed potatoes, or, in the French manner, with maca-roni dressed with the meat gravy and grated Parmesan.

*Serves 6*

2½ pounds boneless chuck, trimmed
   of excess fat and cut into 2-inch
   cubes

### The Marinade (Optional):

1 onion, sliced

2 carrots, scrubbed and sliced

4 garlic cloves, chopped

1 celery rib, chopped

1 cup full-bodied red wine

1 tablespoon sugar

1 tablespoon dried thyme leaves

2 bay leaves

### The Meat Braise:

flour for dredging

salt and freshly ground pepper to taste

1 2-inch piece of beef suet

1½ cups full-bodied red wine

3 cups homemade or condensed
   canned (undiluted) beef broth

1 cup V-8 tomato cocktail (not spicy)

### The Vegetables:

6 medium new potatoes, peeled and
   halved

6 carrots, quartered, or 18 ready-to-
   cook baby carrots

12 small white boiling onions, peeled

Marinating the meat will produce a more deeply flavorful stew, but you can skip this step. Place the meat in a bowl with the combined marinade ingredients, cover, and refrigerate overnight.

Preheat the oven to 350°. Remove the meat from the marinade, reserving the drained vegetables. Drain and blot the meat on paper towels and toss the cubes in a plastic bag with a small amount of flour, salt, and pepper. Shake off the excess. Put the suet in a large heavy skillet and render it over medium-high heat for a couple of minutes, until a glaze of fat covers the pan surface. Leave the suet in the center and place the beef cubes around it so they don't touch. Brown the meat in 3 batches, for about 6 minutes each, turning the cubes once. Transfer the meat to a covered dutch oven or ovenproof casserole.

Layer in the marinade vegetables or use freshly prepared ones if you skipped that step. Add the wine to the hot skillet and let it sizzle for a minute to deglaze the pan. Add the broth and V-8 and scrape up all the caramelized bits from the skillet. Pour the liquid over the meat, cover the casserole, and oven-braise the meat for 3 hours.

Transfer the meat to a bowl with tongs, knocking off the vegetables, which should be discarded. Strain the braising liquid back over the meat and, when it has cooled to room temperature, cover and refrigerate overnight. The next day, remove any congealed fat from the top.

Reheat the meat in the broth and, if the sauce isn't thick enough, mix 2 tablespoons soft butter with 2 tablespoons flour and stir the *beurre manié* into the sauce to thicken. Steam the vegetables in a steamer or the microwave and add to the meat. You can do this earlier in the day.

> *If the casserole lid isn't a tight fit, you can seal it with a stiff mixture of flour and water or a layer of foil.*

> *If suet isn't available from your butcher, use 2 tablespoons butter and 1 tablespoon oil.*

> *Cooking the vegetables separately is the best way to avoid overcooking them and producing a watery sauce for the stew.*

> *You can braise the stew on top of the stove over very low heat using a Flame-Tamer.*

> *Stew just gets better and better the longer it keeps, and the cooked meat freezes well. You can braise double the amount of meat, freeze it, and simply steam vegetables or cook noodles for a quick meal.*

> *Frozen stocks are appearing regularly in specialty food stores—often in space-saving concentrated form. Look for them. Perfect Additions is a good one.*

# The All-American Hamburger

*S*urely we were all born knowing how to make and flip a burger—it's in the genes. Why, then, are so many mediocre burgers sizzling away out there? In the interest of preserving a national treasure, we thought a refresher course in the basics might be in order.

*Serves 1*

I. THE MEAT: Not just ground beef but ground chuck. Have the butcher grind a chuck roast for you or grind your own in the food processor by processing only a few pieces at a time. Pulse the blade on and off to avoid mangling or pureeing the meat. If your only choice is packaged meat, look for 20 percent fat content.

Form the 6- to 8-ounce patties very gently without slapping the meat together or flattening it down, or you might as well have saved yourself the trouble of grinding it. Wrap the patties in plastic wrap immediately if you're not cooking them right away.

2. THE PAN: A nonstick pan or seasoned cast-iron skillet is best.

3. THE COOKING: The charcoal grill makes the tastiest burger. Whether you cook them outside or in, it will take 4 to 5 minutes on each side for rare, 6 to 7 minutes for medium, and we refuse to acknowledge well done. For skillet burgers, add a little butter to the pan first.

4. THE BUN: Look for bakery buns with a firm but not crusty surface and a nice rich, yeasty flavor. Or use English muffins. Be sure to butter and toast them.

5. ACCOMPANIMENTS: Crispy fries or onions—maybe both.

*FAVORITES*

➤ THE CHEESEBURGER AND BACON CHEESEBURGER: Cheddar, Gruyère, Monterey Jack, fontina, Gouda, mozzarella, blue—they're all good melted on the second side of the hamburger, but if you're cooking it rare, you may need to run the patties under a hot broiler to melt the cheese. You can also put a lid on the skillet for a minute or so to soften it. We think the best solution is to melt the cheese on the toasted buns while the burgers are cooking.

☞ THE CALIFORNIA BURGER:  This can be avocado, onion, and tomato slices, lettuce, and a kind of Russian dressing—or just mayonnaise, lettuce, and tomato.

☞ THE OLD-FASHIONED ONION SLIDER:  Never mind the skinny little burger—just pile up a ton of softly fried onions on a big, fat juicy one.

☞ THE CHILI BURGER:  *With* beans, of course. Sloppy but good.

☞ THE ALICE WATERS (CHEZ PANISSE) BURGER:  Ms. Waters mixes a little minced onion with the meat and tops it with mustard, tomato, and arugula. She serves it on a toasted soft bun brushed with olive oil and garlic.

## Salisbury Steak

Salisbury steak wasn't originally on our list of memorable American classics, but this book held many surprises for us, and this is one we think is worth sharing. Salisbury steak was named for Dr. James Salisbury who thought we'd all be healthier if we ate lots of beef, specifically 3 pounds a day, washed down with quarts of hot water. The dish that evolved was a humdrum mixture of minced beef, onion, parsley, and bread crumbs broiled with bacon bits on top and splashed with a dull mushroom gravy. Certainly not worthy of culinary history, except it's thought to be the forerunner of the all-American hamburger. Just for fun, we tried it—*sans* gravy. Not bad. Since cooking ground beef rare is becoming yet another food taboo, and ground beef is now so lean it's almost flavorless, we decided to have another look at Salisbury steak, updating the seasoning. Very tasty.

*Serves 4*

1½ pounds lean ground beef

2 slices of day-old bread, crumbled

½ medium sweet onion, minced

¼ cup minced parsley

1 tablespoon roasted garlic puree
  (see instructions on page 85)

1 tablespoon minced fresh rosemary
  or 1 teaspoon dried

2 tablespoons extra-virgin olive oil

salt and freshly ground pepper to taste

4 strips of smoky bacon, partially
  cooked and chopped

Mix the beef together well with everything but the bacon. Form into 4 thick ovals and press the bacon into one side only. Broil, bacon side down first, or panfry until cooked through.

➤ *Substitute any herb or seasoning of your choice for the rosemary.*

➤ *Try seasoning the meat with minced jalapeño and ground cumin. Serve it with a dollop of guacamole (page 12).*

# Chili con Carne

*E*verything from raisins to tomatoes to beans to peanut butter turns up in chili, but this classic Texas bowl of red is pure and simple—and addictive. It's even more delicious the next day, when it will also be a little spicier, so go easy on the cayenne.

In Texas they love to serve saltines with chili—some typical Texas garnishes are listed, but of course you can add sour cream, grated cheese, diced avocado, or snipped cilantro.

*Serves 8*

3 strips of bacon

1 large onion, chopped

8 garlic cloves, unpeeled

4 pounds boneless chuck roast, cut
    into ¼-inch dice or coarsely ground

½ cup mild ground red chile,
    preferably New Mexican

1 tablespoon ground cumin

2 teaspoons dried oregano leaves

1 teaspoon cider vinegar

½ cup strong brewed coffee or
    1 tablespoon instant coffee powder

3 cups beef broth or water as needed

salt to taste

cayenne pepper to taste

2 tablespoons cornmeal

**The Garnish:**

broken saltines

chopped jalapeños

minced onion

In a dutch oven over medium heat, fry the bacon until it's golden and set aside for a cook's treat. Add the onion and cook until soft. Smash the garlic cloves with the flat side of a chef's knife, discard the peel, and add the smashed cloves to the onion. Sauté until transparent.

Add the meat in thirds along with the chile, cumin, and oregano. Stir until it browns, then add the vinegar, coffee, and enough stock or water just to cover the meat. Cover the pot and cook over low heat for 2 hours, stirring occasionally. Remove the lid for a final hour of cooking over medium heat—the chili should simmer. Taste for salt and add the cayenne if you're using it—½ teaspoon will provide a lot of heat. Add the cornmeal and stir it in well. Cook for 15 minutes more.

Serve the chili in deep bowls with garnishes for each guest to add at the table.

☞ *Ask the butcher for chili-grind chuck. Or talk him into cutting chuck roast into dice or do it yourself; Texans claim the little cubes make a vastly superior chili, and we think the extra fuss is worth it.*

☞ *If you can't find real ground chile, you can either grind chile peppers in the food processor or spice grinder, removing veins and seeds first, or look for a good chili powder, such as Gebhardt's.*

# Black Bean Chili

his is a streamlined version of the superb vegetarian chili developed at the famous Greens restaurant in San Francisco by founding chef Deborah Madison. You could cut the recipe in half for 4 people, but then you wouldn't have any leftovers, and you'd be sorry.

*Serves 8*

2 cups dried black turtle beans,
   soaked overnight
1 bay leaf
3 tablespoons corn or peanut oil
3 medium yellow onions, cut into
   ¼-inch dice
4 garlic cloves, coarsely chopped
½ teaspoon salt
4 teaspoons ground cumin
4 teaspoons dried oregano leaves

4 teaspoons paprika
½ teaspoon cayenne pepper
¼ cup mild ground red chile,
   preferably New Mexican
1½ pounds diced canned tomatoes,
   preferably organic, undrained
1 to 2 teaspoons chopped dried or
   canned chipotle chile or jalapeño
1 tablespoon rice wine vinegar
¼ cup chopped cilantro

**The Garnish:**

grated Muenster cheese
diced fresh or canned green chiles

sour cream
cilantro sprigs

Drain the soaked beans and put them in a dutch oven. Cover them with fresh water by a couple of inches, add the bay leaf, and bring to a boil. Lower the heat and simmer, uncovered, while you prepare the rest of the ingredients.

Heat the oil in a large skillet over medium heat and sauté the onions until soft. Add the garlic, salt, cumin, oregano, paprika, cayenne, and ground chile and cook for 5 minutes. Add the tomatoes with their liquid and 1 teaspoon of the chipotle chile.

Simmer for 15 minutes, then add this mixture to the beans—the beans should be covered with an inch of liquid; add water to that level if necessary. Continue cooking the beans slowly until they're soft, an hour or longer. Keep an eye on the water level and add more if necessary to keep the beans well covered.

When the beans are cooked, taste them—they may need more chipotle. Season to taste with the vinegar, additional salt if needed, and the chopped cilantro. Serve the chili in deep bowls over a mound of grated cheese and add the garnishes on top.

*Chipotle chiles come dried or canned in adobo sauce. They're the smoked version of jalapeños, and the canned version is such a wonderful condiment to have on hand that it's worth seeking out. Puree the canned chiles and keep them in the refrigerator; they'll last for months, and a little dollop will enliven a number of dishes.*

*You could speed things up by cooking the beans in a pressure cooker (30 minutes at 15 pounds) or using canned black beans. If you use organic canned beans and rinse them well, you'll get something very tasty, though the texture won't be as good.*

*This chili is versatile; it can go into enchiladas or be thinned out with water or stock for black bean soup. You can also puree it to make an excellent dip for vegetables or tortilla chips. It freezes well, so it's worth making a double recipe.*

# Moussaka

oussaka is such a multinational favorite that we Americans might as well lay our claim to it right along with the Greeks, Turks, Serbs, and Croats. It's a first cousin to eggplant parmigiana, made with ground lamb instead of beef. Moussaka fills the house with the aroma of cinnamon and allspice that's so distinctive in Middle Eastern savories. Like most layered and baked dishes, this one develops its full flavor by the second day and keeps so well you should make the full recipe and enjoy it twice.

We voted to use a simpler creamy topping than the extra-step *saltsa besamel*. If your love of eggplant doesn't justify the salting, draining, and cooking, layer the moussaka instead with thinly sliced potatoes.

*Serves 6*

3 medium eggplants
salt

olive oil

**The Meat Sauce:**

2 tablespoons olive oil
1 large onion, chopped
3 garlic cloves, minced
salt and freshly ground pepper
   to taste
½ teaspoon ground cinnamon
¼ teaspoon ground allspice

1½ pounds ground lamb or beef
1 cup tomato sauce, preferably Muir
   Glen or Contadina
½ cup dry red wine (optional)
2 tablespoons tomato paste (tube
   paste is easier)
¼ cup chopped parsley

**The Topping:**

1 cup sour cream
1 cup plain yogurt, drained

pinch of freshly grated nutmeg
¼ cup grated Parmesan cheese

**CLASSIC AMERICAN FOOD WITHOUT FUSS**

Peel and thinly slice the eggplant lengthwise. Salt the slices and let them drain in a colander for an hour. Rinse off the salt and pat the slices dry. Arrange the eggplant on a broiler rack, brush both sides liberally with olive oil, and broil close to the heat until brown streaks appear and the flesh softens. Do not overcook, or the eggplant will fall apart. You can also shallow-fry the eggplant in considerably more oil.

Preheat the oven to 350° and prepare the meat sauce. Heat the oil in a large skillet and sauté the onion and garlic until they soften. Add the seasonings and meat and break up the lumps by pressing down with the back of a wooden spoon. When no red remains in the meat, add the rest of the ingredients and simmer the sauce over medium-low heat for 15 to 20 minutes. Taste for seasonings.

Mix together the topping ingredients. Alternately layer the eggplant, then the meat sauce in a shallow ovenproof serving dish. Spread the topping over it and bake for 1 hour.

## Shashlik

*Along with the fifties mania for outdoor cookery came our discovery of shashlik, or shish kebab, an old-world favorite of our own coastal Russian immigrants from the Caucasus. Typically we had to make it less "foreign," and soon we were impaling all sorts of mongrel combinations like cubes of canned ham and pineapple with green bell pepper, brushed with honey and mustard. For this 3,000-year-old study in simplicity, you need only marinate lamb loin cubes (or beef, pork, chicken, or game) in cooking oil, lemon juice or vinegar, grated onion, salt, pepper, garlic, parsley, and dill or oregano for a couple of hours at room temperature. Thread the cubes on long skewers with small onion quarters and squares of green pepper, both briefly steamed in the microwave. Grill over charcoal, basting frequently, for about 15 minutes and serve over rice pilaf garnished with ripe tomato wedges and minced scallions.*

# Texas Oven-Barbecued Lamb Shanks

*O*ne of our favorite cookbook photo captions found in the course of researching this book reads: "Lamb shanks stuffed with barley will appeal to the clever hostess for the rumpus room dinner." That was 1947, and although sometimes we feel as though we're always cooking for the rumpus room dinner, everyone seems to have forgotten about lamb shanks—unless they're French style, with lots of garlic and red wine. In the West, however, lamb of all kinds has always been more popular (maybe it was those Basque shepherds in Nevada), and you can still find these oven-barbecued shanks there.

If you're not used to cooking lamb shanks, look for the hind shanks, which are meatier—and if they look a little too Stone Age for you, consider asking the butcher to crack them in 3 places, which will make them easier to cook. Don't be deterred; lamb shanks are delectable, and once you taste them, you'll cook them often.

*Serves 6*

2 medium onions, finely chopped

1 cup ketchup

2 cups water

½ cup cider vinegar

1 tablespoon Worcestershire sauce

2 teaspoons dry mustard, preferably
   Colman's

3 garlic cloves, smashed (see page 112)

1 teaspoon salt

1 teaspoon freshly ground pepper

¼ cup packed dark brown sugar

½ teaspoon cayenne pepper

¼ cup strong black coffee

6 lamb shanks

Bring all the ingredients except lamb to a boil in a saucepan; reduce the heat and simmer for 25 minutes, stirring from time to time.

Preheat the oven to 325°. Arrange the shanks in a roasting pan with a tight lid.

Pour the barbecue sauce over and cover the pan. Roast for 2 hours, basting from time to time and turning the shanks at least once, until the meat is fork-tender. Transfer them to a heated serving platter and keep warm for 15 minutes.

> *If you like, you can take the meat off the bones before serving it.*

> *The truth is, there are some excellent not-too-sweet barbecue sauces on the market, and you can save yourself some time by using them, doctored up or not. You can add coffee and dry mustard to approximate this recipe. You might need a jolt of hot sauce here too.*

> *Some recipes suggest removing the thin plasticlike membrane that covers the shanks, but it's not necessary.*

> *If you want to make French-style shanks, brown them all over in a little olive oil before they go into the oven. Toss in a few garlic cloves, sprinkle with salt and pepper, strew some herbes de Provence over them, and add 2 cups of full-bodied red wine. After the first hour, add a dozen peeled shallots per person. When the shanks are cooked, pour off any fat from the sauce and reduce the sauce over medium-high heat if necessary. Pour the sauce over the shanks and serve.*

> *You can also brown lamb shanks under the broiler; salt and pepper them, then broil 5 minutes on each side, and proceed with the recipe.*

# Irish Stew

This easiest of all stews is a so-called white stew—the meat isn't browned first, no flour is added, and the vegetables are all white. Originally it was made with mutton, but shoulder lamb chops are just right. The traditional Irish stew has no seasoning except salt and pepper, but here we've added bay leaf, parsley, garlic, and whole cloves, the inspiration of Maxim's restaurant in Paris, of all places.

Like all stews, it's much better made a day or two ahead of serving. Remove any lamb fat congealed on the surface before reheating. And if there seems to be too much liquid, cook uncovered a little longer, to reduce it.

This recipe is for 6 people, but you can scale it up or down—just remember to use 1 shoulder chop, 1 baking potato, and ½ onion per person.

*Serves 6*

6 shoulder lamb chops, up to 1 inch
    thick
6 baking potatoes, sliced
3 yellow onions, sliced
½ cup chopped parsley
salt and freshly ground pepper
    to taste

2 garlic cloves, chopped
2 bay leaves
3 cloves
1 cup homemade (page 25) or
    canned chicken broth
½ cup dry bread crumbs for garnish
    (optional)

Preheat the oven to 325°. Trim the chops of all visible fat and cut them into thirds, including the circle of bone for flavor. In an ovenproof casserole with a tight-fitting lid, assemble the stew in layers, beginning and ending with potatoes: potatoes, onions, parsley, lamb. Season each layer with salt and pepper as you go. Tuck in garlic pieces and the cloves and bay leaves here and there. Finish with a top layer of potatoes.

Pour the broth over the entire casserole and set it in the oven, tightly covered, to cook for 2 hours or until everything is tender. Chill the stew overnight or for a couple of days.

Remove any fat that has congealed on the surface and fish out the bay leaves and cloves. When ready to serve, reheat the stew in the oven for 30 minutes or until hot. To dress up this humble fare, scatter the bread crumbs on top of the casserole and spoon a little of the cooking liquid over them. Run the casserole under the broiler until the crumbs are crispy. Serve the stew in hot soup plates.

*Don't skimp on the pepper—this stew needs lots.*

*The traditional stew is served with boiled carrots on the side.*

*You can add carrots, parsnips, even turnips if you like. But try the unvarnished version first—it's delectable.*

# Stuffed Pork Chops

The thought of stuffed pork chops is a warm and fuzzy one, but the stuffing doesn't inspire nostalgic longings or spur any debate among aficionados. There are innumerable stuffing possibilities, but we think the best marriage is between pork and fruit, so we've settled on a classic bread filling with dried apples and a few optional pecans for crunch. What makes this version memorable is the apple bits in the sauce along with the bite of creamed horseradish. The perfect accompaniment is thick quarters of baked sweet potatoes sautéed in just enough butter to caramelize the outside, leaving the inside creamy soft.

*Serves 4*

4 slices of fresh homemade-style bread

4 thick loin or rib pork chops with a single bone

4 shallots, finely minced

1/4 cup chopped Sunsweet dried apple bits plus 1/4 cup for the sauce

1/4 cup chopped toasted pecans (optional)

2 tablespoons minced parsley

1 teaspoon ground allspice

1 teaspoon dried thyme leaves

salt and freshly ground pepper to taste

2 tablespoons heavy cream plus 1/2 cup for the sauce

2 tablespoons butter

1 1/2 cups apple juice

1 tablespoon Inglehoffer cream horseradish

2 tablespoons snipped chives

Pull the bread slices into small bits with your fingers and spread them out in a single layer to dry. If you haven't time to wait, or it's a humid day, tuck the bread crumbs into a toaster oven on low heat until most of the moisture evaporates. Don't let them become hard.

Using a sharp, preferably curved-blade knife, cut pockets in the chops by making a 2-inch slit in the side opposite the bone and cutting straight down to it. Then angle the knife, cutting to the right and left to make a large pocket but keeping the opening small. This will prevent the filling from popping out—but don't worry if a little of it does. You can just spoon it on top of the chops when they're done.

Combine all the stuffing ingredients, starting with the shallots and finishing with a couple of tablespoons of cream, more or less. The stuffing should just hold together lightly without compacting. Press a quarter of the stuffing into each chop, being certain to fill the whole pocket generously so that the chops look fat and plump when you're finished. Heat the butter in a sauté pan with a lid and add the chops just before the butter starts to brown. Push a toothpick standing straight up in the middle of the slit, stopping when the point hits the pan. Cook the chops quickly on one side until they have attractive golden patches on the surface. Turn them over, pulling out the pick and reinserting new ones, and cook the second side until golden. Leaving the picks in place, pour in just 1 cup of the apple juice, put the lid on the pan, and lower the heat to braise the chops for about 20 minutes.

When you lift the lid, you will note that the apple juice has evaporated by about half and what remains is a dark, sticky glaze. Transfer the cooked chops to a warm platter and add the extra ½ cup of apple juice along with the ¼ cup of apple bits, boiling it down rapidly for a few seconds while scraping up the caramelized juices. Add the creamed horseradish, snipped chives, and the rest of the heavy cream, and reduce the sauce again until it is nicely thickened. It should be a rich, glossy brown. Distribute the chunky sauce over the chops and serve immediately.

*For mushroom stuffing, substitute dried mushrooms for the apple bits in the stuffing and delete the pecans and allspice. Use chicken broth instead of apple juice for braising and sauté quartered fresh cremini mushrooms for the sauce.*

# Oven-Barbecued Spareribs

*L*ots of people think spareribs are hopelessly complicated to cook at home, but these are both easy and delicious. They're also available year-round since they don't depend on grilling.

We're not fans of the parboiling technique of cooking ribs—these are just given a preliminary rub. When they're done, they should be just separating from the bone at the first bite.

You can sauce the ribs or not, as you like. If you use the sauce on ribs grilled outdoors, don't brush it on until the last 20 minutes of cooking, so it won't burn.

*Serves 6*

2 sides of trimmed spareribs, 1 pound
   per person, at room temperature

**Rib Rub:**

1 tablespoon salt

1 tablespoon freshly ground pepper

1 teaspoon ground white pepper

⅛ cup paprika

2 tablespoons light brown sugar

**The Barbecue Sauce:**

1 teaspoon chili powder, such as
   Gebhardt's

1 teaspoon celery seeds

¼ cup packed dark brown sugar

¼ cup cider vinegar

¼ cup Worcestershire sauce

1 cup ketchup

1 cup water

2 tablespoons butter

several drops of liquid smoke
   (optional)

Trim the transparent sheet off the backs of the ribs by pulling it down using a paper towel. Mix the rub ingredients in a small bowl. Rub the meat all over with the mixed rib rub and let stand for 2 hours. Put the ribs in a shallow roasting pan. Preheat the oven to 350°. Put the ribs in the oven and roast for 45 minutes.

Meanwhile, combine all the sauce ingredients in a saucepan and simmer for 20 minutes. Remove the ribs from the oven after 45 minutes and drain off all the drippings. Baste the drained ribs with the sauce, return the pan to the oven, and lower the heat to 300°. Bake for 1 hour and 15 minutes longer, basting from time to time with the sauce.

➣ *For outdoor ribs, we like Charleston cook John Taylor's minimalist version: He just salts and peppers the ribs and leaves them on a platter to come to room temperature. When the ribs go on the grill, he adds 2 whole heads of garlic per person to the coals below and covers the grill. The ribs cook for 30 minutes on each side. When they're done—they may take longer— they're cut into serving pieces. The heads of roasted garlic are sliced open at the base, and the soft garlic is squeezed out and rubbed all over the ribs. Sensational and about the easiest barbecue in the world. You can also make this garlic puree in the oven; put the garlic, wrapped in foil, in a 350° oven for 1 hour.*

➣ *Of course you can season the ribs ahead, even a day ahead; the flavor will only improve.*

➣ *Country ribs are meatier; serve just ½ pound per person. Baby back ribs are charming but don't have as much flavor as the big ribs.*

➣ *If you don't want to fuss with a sauce, try Kraft Hickory Smoked Barbecue Sauce—just add a little cider vinegar, a little powdered instant coffee, whatever seems interesting.*

# Sausages and Peppers

*R*egions without a serious Italian community may not have sausages and peppers on their tables. If that's you, run out and make this dish, and it will appear regularly from your kitchen—we promise.

The sausages can be sweet or hot, with fennel seeds or without, but they're always fresh Italian sausages, broiled, grilled, or cooked in a skillet, then combined with the peppers. The only trick here is to remember to start the peppers well ahead—it seems as though they'd cook very quickly, but it takes a good half hour.

*Serves 4*

¼ cup olive oil

2 garlic cloves

2 onions, sliced

6 bell peppers, green, red, or a
    mixture, cut into 1-inch-
    wide slices

8 sweet or hot Italian sausages,
    about 2 pounds

Heat the oil in a large skillet over medium heat. Smash the garlic with the side of a chef's knife, slip off the skin, and cook until the garlic begins to brown; remove and discard it. Add the onions and cook until soft, stirring from time to time so they cook evenly. Don't let them brown. Add the peppers and salt to taste, stir them well, and cover. Cook the peppers over low heat until they're soft, about 30 minutes.

Meanwhile, cook the sausages. Prick them all over with a fork and either broil them until they're golden, grill them, or cook them in another skillet over medium heat with several tablespoons of water, turning them so they cook evenly. It will take about 15 minutes for the water to evaporate and the sausages to cook.

When the sausages are done and the peppers are ready, mix them together and cook for about 5 minutes to blend the flavors. Serve with crusty Italian bread.

## Veal Scaloppine

*Nothing could be quicker or more versatile. We regret seeing this classic slide into oblivion. Maybe the admonition that the well-prepared scaloppine should never hit the pan scares off the home cook. The only trick is to use first-quality veal and literally flash-cook the thin pieces. Use good olive oil in a hot steel-lined aluminum skillet. Season the scallops well with salt and freshly ground pepper and have everything else ready to serve. The veal will take only about a minute on each side. Squeeze lemon juice over the finished scaloppine or sprinkle both sides with freshly grated Parmesan for the last second of each turn or simply splash some Marsala or dry vermouth into the empty pan and reduce it while scraping up any browned bits, and then drizzle it over the scallops.*

# Ossobuco alla Gremolata

hat's so unforgettable about gently braised veal shanks? It's the succulent texture of the tender meat and the aromatic pan glaze that slithers over those shanks like a satin "teddy." As seductive as its Italian homeland, ossobuco combines soul satisfaction and visual allure—and it's so easy on the cook. Don't ignore the delectable marrow nestled in the center of the bone.

*Serves 4*

4 meaty 1½-inch veal shanks (hind
    shanks are meatiest)

2 tablespoons butter

2 tablespoons olive oil

salt and freshly ground pepper to taste

½ medium onion, finely chopped

1 small carrot, grated

pinch of dried rosemary

2 tablespoons tomato paste (tube
    paste is easiest)

1 cup dry white wine or more as
    needed

½ cup homemade or canned veal,
    beef, or chicken broth, or more as
    needed

2 tablespoons minced flat-leaf parsley

grated zest of 1 lemon

2 teaspoons minced garlic

Tie a piece of kitchen string around the perimeter of each shank to hold the meat against the bone. Choose a covered sauté pan in which the shanks just fit with the sides touching. Sauté them on both sides over medium-high heat in the butter and oil until they're nicely colored. Salt and pepper them liberally. Remove the shanks from the pan and sauté the onion and carrot until it softens. Sprinkle in a little rosemary and add back the meat along with the tomato paste mixed with the wine and the broth. Cover the pan tightly and reduce the heat so that the liquid simmers very

gently, adding more broth and wine whenever needed. The shanks must cook slowly for about 2 hours or until the meat falls away from the bone and is fork-tender.

Transfer the meat to a plate, keeping it warm while you reduce the pan juices by half over medium-high heat. If there isn't enough left to sauce the meat well, add more beef broth and wine. Garnish each serving with the gremolata, a mixture of the parsley, grated lemon zest, and garlic.

&#10148; *Ossobuco is traditionally served with risotto Milanese (see page 145).*

&#10148; *Do not attempt to reheat ossobuco. Veal dries out unpleasantly when reheated. You can make it a short time ahead, leave it in the covered pan, and gently bring it back to serving temperature later.*

&#10148; *Instead of the tomato paste, you can use a 1-pound can of imported Italian plum tomatoes, drained and chopped, or vine-ripened tomatoes, peeled, seeded, and chopped. If you put up slow-roasted tomatoes from the previous summer in your freezer, they would work perfectly too.*

&#10148; *There's an authentic "white" version of ossobuco, i.e., without tomato. Simply use white wine and a rich homemade chicken broth to braise the meat.*

&#10148; *Try adding a couple of mashed anchovies to the gremolata.*

&#10148; *We like chopped fennel added to this recipe. To complement the anise flavor of fennel, add 6 thin orange zest strips to the broth.*

&#10148; *If you have room for a couple of extra shanks in the pan, by all means cook them. The meat and marrow make a wonderful ragù for pasta with a little cream to thin it out—or mince the meat along with a few sautéed mushrooms to make a delicious filling for ravioli.*

# Duck à l'Orange

Although other cultures prepare duck in various wonderful ways, Americans favor the traditional French roast with orange sauce or the fabulous crispy Peking duck of China. Since there is no truly simple way to cook Peking duck, we're offering our Berlitz à l'orange version, with an apologetic wink at the chefs at Lasserre. Duck à l'orange without fuss? The truth is that roasting a duck is no fussier than roasting a chicken. It may seem daunting because it's a restaurant classic, but fear not; it's easily prepared at home. There are only four reasonably simple things to strive for: crisp skin, moist meat, minimal fat, and a citrus sauce nicely balanced between sweet and sour. This recipe does the trick, using a vertical poultry roasting rack. If you have one, it's probably been shoved to the back of the cupboard. Using the rack is the secret to a crispy duck.

*Serves 4*

**The Orange Sauce:**

2 tablespoons sugar

1 tablespoon balsamic vinegar

1 tablespoon red wine vinegar

1 navel orange

2 tablespoons frozen orange juice
   concentrate

¼ teaspoon salt and freshly ground
   pepper

pinch of cayenne pepper

1 cup homemade (page 125) or
   canned duck, chicken, or beef broth

1 teaspoon arrowroot mixed with
   1 tablespoon water

**The Duck:**

1 5-pound Long Island duckling,
   rinsed and dried

1 tablespoon dark soy sauce

2 teaspoons honey

¼ cup dry red wine

In a small saucepan, slowly simmer the sugar and vinegars until the mixture becomes a thick, caramelized syrup. Remove the zest of half the orange and cut into thin strips. Section the rest and set aside. Whisk the orange juice concentrate, salt, pepper, cayenne, and orange zest into the syrup. Add the broth and simmer the sauce for about 15 minutes. Taste and adjust. Strain the sauce and keep it on an unlit back burner until the duck is finished or make it a day or two ahead, refrigerate, and reheat. The arrowroot mixture will be added to thicken the sauce just before serving.

As soon as you bring the duck home, wash it, blot it dry, and store it in the refrigerator, uncovered, for up to 3 days. The skin will shrink and feel like parchment paper, which will assure its crispiness.

Preheat the oven to 350°. Brush the duck all over with a mixture of the soy and honey. Prick the skin well at the joint where the leg meets the breast and position the duck on a vertical roaster rack in a small nonstick roasting pan. Tuck a piece of foil over the neck and breast only. Slide the duck onto the center rack of the oven and roast for 45 minutes.

Pull the duck from the oven, remove the foil, and draw off most of the fat from the pan with a bulb baster. Prick the skin once again between the breast and thigh. Return the duck to the oven and roast for another 30 minutes. The duck will be mahogany colored and the skin beautifully crisp.

Transfer the duck to a cutting board. Pour off as much fat as possible without disturbing the pan drippings and duck juices. With the roasting pan over medium-low heat and the drippings bubbling, pour in the wine and scrape it all together. Whisk it into the orange sauce, thicken the sauce with the arrowroot, and add the orange segments just to warm them. Carve the duck in serving slices. Ladle some of the sauce over each serving of carved meat and garnish with orange segments. There's no better accompaniment for duck à l'orange than wild rice with sautéed shallots.

*Williams-Sonoma carries a line of wonderful Austrian fruit syrups by d'Arbo, one of which is Mandarinen Sirup, made with tangerine concentrate* and sugar. Use all red wine vinegar and no balsamic and ¼ cup of the syrup in place of the orange juice concentrate and orange zest. It makes a wonderful intense sauce. Call (800) 541-2233 for mail order or the store nearest you.

➣ D'Artagnan duck demi-glace, among others, is much better than canned broth. It can be found in specialty stores or bought by mail order: (800) 327-8246.

➣ One duck for two people leaves just enough pickings to tuck in the freezer for the world's best fried rice.

# Chicken with
# 40 Cloves of Garlic

This dish had a hard time getting out of Provence, its native home. In London in the early part of this century they could scarcely believe a person could eat so much garlic and live, and in America James Beard created a sensation on "The Garry Moore Show" when he revealed how much garlic was in the dish—it was the fifties, and we hadn't yet fallen in love with garlic. This intensely fragrant mellow chicken gives you a lot of mileage for virtually no work at all. It's also one of the few dishes we can think of that doesn't require peeling the garlic first.

*Serves 6*

12 chicken thighs
salt and freshly ground pepper to taste
3 heads of garlic, separated into
   cloves

1 parsley sprig, chopped
1 teaspoon herbes de Provence
¼ cup olive oil

Preheat the oven to 350°. Arrange the chicken thighs in a dutch oven and salt and pepper them. In a bowl, mix the remaining ingredients and spoon over the chicken. Seal the pot with a sheet of foil to seal tightly so the garlic won't burn, cover, and bake for 1 hour and 15 minutes. Serve with toasted French bread to smear with the garlic—mashed potatoes are perfect with this.

# Fried Chicken

*P*roperly prepared, this is one of the most delectable dishes imaginable. If you've had only greasy, pasty fried chicken, you'll be amazed at how crisp and succulent this chicken is. Fried right, the chicken will absorb almost none of the grease. This is classic Southern deep-fried chicken, but you can also panfry it or even oven-fry it (see the end of the recipe).

| | |
|---|---|
| 1 3- to 4-pound frying chicken, cut up, or 8 pieces of chicken | 1 cup flour |
| lard, peanut oil, or vegetable shortening mixed with bacon fat for deep frying | 1 teaspoon salt |
| | 1 teaspoon freshly ground pepper |
| | 1/4 teaspoon cayenne pepper or paprika (optional) |

*Serves 4*

Rinse and dry the chicken. Put the oil or fat in a large heavy pot—a dutch oven is perfect—over medium heat. The fat shouldn't come more than halfway up the sides of the pot but should be deep enough so that the chicken pieces can float on it.

While the oil is heating, put the remaining ingredients in a paper bag and shake well to mix them. One piece at a time, drop the chicken into the bag and shake well to coat it thoroughly.

When the fat reaches 370°—test with a thermometer or flick a drop of water in to see if it sputters—it's ready. Start with the dark meat—legs and thighs—since they'll take a few more minutes to cook. Arrange the chicken in the pot, being careful not to crowd the pieces. Don't let the temperature get over 375° or under 365° while the chicken cooks, about 20 minutes. When it's golden brown all over and tender—check with a fork—it's ready.

Have some paper bags ready for draining the chicken or a rack set over a baking sheet. Remove the chicken pieces with tongs and let them drain. Grind some fresh pepper over the chicken and sprinkle a little salt on too. Scrape up and discard any bits on the bottom of the pan and bring the fat back to 370° before continuing with the next batch of chicken.

When you're finished, filter the fat through a coffee filter before storing it—you can use it a second time.

✒ TO PANFRY CHICKEN: *It's a good idea to soak the chicken in buttermilk for an hour or so before dipping it in the seasoned flour. Add the fat to the halfway mark on an electric frying pan or a cast-iron skillet and heat over medium heat. When the temperature reaches 375°, add the chicken pieces. Fry 15 or 20 minutes, until golden brown. Reduce the heat to 350°, turn the chicken with tongs, and fry for another 15 minutes, until golden brown. Drain as usual.*

✒ CHICKEN À LA MARYLAND: *No one seems quite sure what this dish actually entails beyond cream gravy with fried chicken. But here's how to make cream gravy: Soak the chicken in 1 cup half-and-half or milk for an hour; reserve the milk. Reserve a couple of tablespoons of the seasoned flour. Pour off all but a couple of tablespoons of the fat left in the skillet. Scrape up all the tasty little bits that stick to the bottom. Put the skillet over medium heat and add the flour, stirring and cooking until it starts to brown. Add the reserved milk, continuing to stir and cook. When the gravy has reached the consistency you want, taste for salt and pepper, season, and serve immediately.*

✒ TO OVEN-FRY: *Preheat the oven to 375°. Meanwhile, melt ¼ pound (1 stick) butter on a large baking sheet with a rim. When the butter is melted, dip the chicken pieces in it and coat them with butter. Drop the chicken pieces, one at a time, into the bag with the seasoned flour as directed, then place them skin side down on the baking sheet. Bake for 45 minutes, turn, and bake for another 5 to 10 minutes, until the top crust looks bubbly. Serve hot or at room temperature—the drippings make good gravy.*

# Roast Chicken

*A* perfectly roasted chicken is an absolute joy—and a rarity. Like all very simple dishes, it depends on a combination of first-rate ingredients and attentive cooking. Every now and then we get a wonderful chicken and, yes, it's more likely to be a free-range chicken, but we've also had tasteless free-range clunkers as well as some delicious chickens from the industrial chicken farms. Look for a chicken with some fat under the skin, a wide meaty breast, and good color—by which we mean creamy ivory, not bright yellow.

This high-heat-roasted chicken is based on Barbara Kafka's famous recipe, which is not only the easiest and fastest but definitely the best. You don't truss it, you don't stuff it, and in fact you spend just a moment or two on this chicken and reap huge rewards: a crisp-skinned bird with great juices that smells utterly delectable. Be sure your oven is clean before you start, to avoid setting off the smoke alarm—there will be smoke, and a messy oven.

*Serves 4*

1 5- to 6-pound roasting chicken,
    wing tips snipped off
salt and freshly ground pepper to taste

1 lemon, cut in half
4 garlic cloves

Bring the chicken to room temperature. Preheat the oven to 500°.

Rinse and dry the chicken inside and out. Pull out any extra fat in the cavity and under the rump. Put the chicken on a shallow rack inside a baking dish just slightly larger than the chicken. Salt and pepper the cavity and insert the lemon and garlic. Sprinkle salt and pepper all over the chicken.

Put the chicken in the oven legs first on the second-lowest rack setting and roast for 50 to 60 minutes or until a leg moves easily when you try it.

Transfer the chicken from the oven to a serving platter. Turn it on its breast to rest for 10 minutes so that the juices return to the breast (which tends to dry out in roasting).

Meanwhile, remove all but a tablespoon or two of fat from the roasting juices. Scrape up all the tasty bits in the pan. Taste for seasoning; you can either simply spoon the juices over the sliced chicken or make a simple gravy by adding 1 cup hot chicken broth and a spoonful of instant flour and cooking the gravy down right in the roasting pan for a few minutes over medium heat.

Turn the chicken right side up, add any juices that have escaped back to the cooking juices, and serve, surrounded by sprigs of watercress or parsley.

*For a little more flavor (and just a little more fuss) you can season the bird under the skin before it goes in the oven. Mix a couple of tablespoons of softened butter with some minced lemon zest, some thyme, and a little pressed garlic. With your fingers, carefully loosen the skin over the breast and wiggle in some of the butter so that it can baste the chicken from the inside.*

*Other seasoning options: a couple of sprigs of rosemary in the cavity or a whole head of garlic, an onion and a quartered orange in the cavity, an olive oil rub all over, followed by salt and pepper.*

## Jerk Chicken

*In Miami and the Keys, this Jamaican favorite—by way of the Arawak Indians—is a classic, and it's gaining national popularity fast. Luckily for the growing cadre of spicy food fanatics, jerk seasoning is now available in jars in gourmet food stores. They say the primary ingredients are onions, thyme, nutmeg, and black pepper, but we know the "jerk man" tosses in a few incendiary scotch bonnet peppers. Marinate chicken parts in the sauce for 30 minutes and grill, pan-sauté in butter and oil, or broil. Serve with pigeon peas and rice and some chilled sliced mango to cool your tongue.*

➤ If the chicken is starting to get too brown, make a foil tent for it and place loosely on top.

➤ If the pan juices are starting to burn, add a little hot water to the pan.

➤ Some recipes suggest tenting the finished chicken with foil to keep it warm before it's served, but French chef Jacques Pepin strongly objects—you'll just be steaming the chicken.

➤ If you have a larger or smaller chicken, just observe the weight: This method requires 10 minutes to the pound. Free-range chickens may take a little longer. Insert the tip of a knife between the thigh and the body to be sure the juices are running clear; if they aren't, the chicken isn't done yet.

➤ A smaller chicken may do better at a lower temperature: A 3-pound chicken can roast at 375° for almost an hour. Brush it first with melted butter.

# Chicken Potpie

*M*aking a chicken potpie from scratch is a little like making lasagne—you combine several recipes, which means hours in the kitchen. But both dishes are so delicious and beloved that they seem worth all the trouble. Still, they can be simplified, and here we offer a few tricks to speed your potpie along.

Although this is a homey, family kind of dinner, try serving it to guests for a casual supper—they'll be overjoyed.

You can make the chicken a day ahead (or buy a roasted chicken) and get the sauce made a day ahead too, so that all you have to do on the day you serve it is put the chicken and sauce together, add the vegetables, and top the pie with the pastry—in this case it's frozen puff pastry from the supermarket, so it's no big deal.

*Serves 6*

2½ pounds chicken breasts and
   thighs

2 to 3 cups homemade (page 125)
   or canned chicken broth

6 tablespoons (¾ stick) butter

6 tablespoons flour

½ teaspoon dried thyme

1¼ cups half-and-half or milk

salt and freshly ground pepper to taste

½ cup frozen pearl onions, thawed

¼ pound cremini mushrooms, sliced

¼ cup diced celery, including some of
   the inner yellow leaves

3 medium carrots, diced

1 cup frozen tiny peas, thawed

1 sheet of frozen puff pastry, thawed

1 large egg, separated

Put the chicken in a microwave-safe dish and pour the chicken broth over it. Cover with plastic wrap and poach in the microwave on HIGH for 12 minutes or until the juices run clear when you pierce the chicken with the tip of a knife. If you're making the chicken ahead, take it off the bone, discard the skin, and wrap tightly in plastic wrap before refrigerating. Strain and reserve the chicken broth.

To make the sauce, keep the broth hot in a small pan on the back of the stove. In a 2-quart saucepan, melt all but a tablespoon of the butter over medium heat and, when it's sizzling, add the flour, whisking well to make a smooth golden paste. Still whisking, gradually add 2 cups of the stock and the thyme. When it's smooth, increase the heat slightly and cook the sauce until it's thickened. Add the half-and-half, whisking again, and cook until the sauce is smooth. Taste for seasoning and add more stock or water if needed. If you're making the sauce ahead, cool it and refrigerate it, then reheat it just before you put the pie together.

To assemble the pie, melt the remaining tablespoon of butter in a large skillet and add the onions, mushrooms, celery, and carrots. Sauté for about 5 minutes or until the vegetables just begin to soften. Add salt and pepper to taste. Cut the chicken into large cubes.

Preheat the oven to 400°. In a large ovenproof casserole or 6 individual ones, mix the chicken and vegetables, including the peas. Pour the warm sauce over and mix everything together well. Fit a sheet of puff pastry over the casserole, sealing it well around the edges with a little beaten egg white. Paint the top with beaten egg yolk. Cut slits on top in a decorative pattern for the steam to escape. Bake for 35 to 40 minutes or until the crust is puffed and golden.

*If you're using leftover or roasted takeout chicken, it's okay to use canned stock for the sauce, but taste the sauce to be sure it's seasoned properly.*

*This is a pure and simple chicken potpie; if you want more, you can add chopped parsley, tarragon, thyme, potatoes, etc.*

*For even more flavor, add an ounce of well-rinsed dried wild mushrooms to the broth while it's heating on a back burner or to the stock while it's cooking if you're using homemade. Remove and chop the mushrooms before you use the broth in the sauce and add them to the potpie with the vegetables.*

# Chicken Cacciatore

*H*ere's a good culinary example of less being more. You need only buy the best chicken, the freshest garlic, the sweetest tomatoes, the snappiest onion, a bell-ringing pepper, and a bottle of Valpolicella.

*Serves 4 to 6*

¼ cup olive oil

1 large onion, chopped

6 garlic cloves, chopped

1 large green bell pepper, chopped

4 chicken thighs

1 whole chicken breast, split

⅔ cup dry Italian red wine

1 tablespoon balsamic vinegar

¼ teaspoon each dried thyme, oregano, and rosemary leaves

1 28-ounce can whole peeled tomatoes, preferably Muir Glen organic or imported Italian plum tomatoes, drained

Heat the olive oil in a skillet large enough to hold all the chicken pieces and sauté the onion, garlic, and green pepper over medium heat for 5 minutes. Transfer the vegetables to a small bowl with a slotted spoon, leaving the oil in the pan.

Sauté the chicken pieces over medium-high heat until they're well colored. Transfer them to a plate. To deglaze the hot skillet, add the wine, scraping up any browned bits from the bottom and swirling the pan to let the alcohol burn off and reduce the wine by half. Add the vinegar, herbs, and tomatoes along with the juice that clings to them. Add the vegetables and browned chicken thighs. Cover the skillet, turn the heat to low, and cook for 20 minutes.

Add the breast halves, cover, and cook for 15 minutes more. Serve with triangles of polenta, dusted with Parmesan cheese and panfried in butter.

# Coq au Vin

*T*here are very elaborate ways of preparing this wonderful dish—the current authentic version involves adding chicken blood to the sauce. But we think this much older and much simpler interpretation described by the great British food writer Elizabeth David in *French Country Cooking* delivers everything we want from this dish.

You can cook the chicken either on top of the stove or in the oven.

*Serves 4*

4 chicken breast halves and 4 chicken legs
salt and freshly ground pepper to taste
fresh lemon juice
3 tablespoons butter plus butter for the shallots
¼ cup brandy

1 bottle of good red wine, such as Mâcon or Beaujolais
12 small shallots, peeled
1 teaspoon sugar
½ pound mushrooms, quartered and sautéed until tender in butter
1 garlic clove

Rub the chicken pieces with salt, pepper, and lemon juice. In a dutch oven or other deep heavy pan, melt the butter and brown the chicken all over in it. Pour the brandy over the chicken and light the sauce with a match—don't worry, this will look dramatic, but it's not dangerous. When the alcohol has burned off—the flames will be gone—add all but ¼ cup of the wine. Cover the pan and set it either over low heat on top of the stove or in a 300° oven for about I hour or until tender when pierced with a fork.

Meanwhile, cook the shallots in a little butter in a skillet until they're golden. Add the remaining wine and the sugar to glaze them. A few minutes before the chicken is ready, put the onions and mushrooms in the pot with it. Smash the garlic clove with the side of a chef's knife, slip off the skin, and add it to the pot. Let the mixture cook a few minutes until you're ready to serve.

Transfer the chicken to a warm serving platter. Take out the onions and mushrooms and keep them warm. Reduce the sauce in the pot over high heat if necessary. Serve the chicken topped with the sauce, onions, and mushrooms.

*Mixed wild mushrooms will give this dish a more complex taste.*

*There's no point in using a terrific wine, but don't just get the cheapest wine you can find, either, since the wine provides the lion's share of the flavor here. If the French reds are pricey, look for an inexpensive California merlot.*

*You can make this dish with a whole 3-pound chicken if you prefer.*

# Shrimp Creole

This is the most famous stew to come out of New Orleans, but its real home is the West Indies. There are lots of shrimp Creole abominations, with floury sauces and drastically overcooked shrimp in a sauce full of tomato paste. But this one is clean and clear, a delectable dish that's amazingly quick to put together.

*Serves 4*

1½ cups long-grain white rice

3 tablespoons olive oil

½ cup chopped onion

3 scallions, including some of the green, sliced into thin rings

½ large green bell pepper, chopped

1 small jalapeño chile, seeded and finely chopped

½ cup chopped celery heart

1 bay leaf

¼ teaspoon each dried thyme leaves, dried oregano leaves, and ground allspice

2 garlic cloves, minced

1 14.5-ounce can Muir Glen diced tomatoes, undrained

salt and freshly ground pepper to taste

1½ pounds shrimp, peeled (don't bother deveining)

fresh lemon juice

Cook the rice while you're making the shrimp—a good way is free boiling: Dump the rice into a lot of boiling salted water as though you were cooking pasta. Cook uncovered for not more than 10 minutes or until it's done, which means still a little al dente. Drain through a strainer in the sink and keep warm in a covered pot in the oven (at the lowest temperature, or heat the oven briefly and then turn it off).

In a large skillet, warm the olive oil over medium-high heat and add the onion, scallions, green pepper, chile, celery, herbs, and garlic. Cook, uncovered, for about 10 minutes or until the vegetables are soft, stirring every now and then.

Add the tomatoes with their liquid and cook for another 10 minutes or until most of the juice has cooked off. Taste for salt and pepper.

Add the shrimp and stir it well with the tomatoes; cook for about 5 minutes or until the shrimp are pink and springy to the touch. Be careful not to overcook them. Remove the bay leaf and taste again for seasoning. Squeeze a little lemon juice over the hot rice, stir it in, and serve the shrimp on top.

## Scampi alla Griglia

What's even better than steak on the "barbie"? The Italians knew the answer was shrimp long before the Aussies, and we've been following the scent for decades. The flavor of shrimp, garlic, and charcoal essence is perennially intoxicating. This recipe is adapted from Maggie Waldron's in *Fire and Smoke*.

*Serves 4 to 6*

4 garlic cloves

¼ teaspoon salt

2 tablespoons minced shallot or
    scallion

hot red pepper flakes to taste

2 tablespoons butter

⅔ cup extra-virgin olive oil

2 pounds jumbo shrimp, peeled, tails
    left on, deveined if necessary

2 tablespoons fresh lemon juice

⅓ cup chopped flat-leaf parsley

Smash the garlic with the side of a chef's knife or cleaver, pick off the skins, and sprinkle with the salt. Mince the garlic. In a large skillet, sauté the minced garlic, shallot, and pepper flakes in the butter until softened. Pour in the olive oil and let it warm slightly off the heat.

Toss the shrimp with the lemon juice and add them to the sauce in the skillet.

Marinate in the sauce for 30 minutes while the coals in the grill are burning down to low embers.

Arrange the shrimp in a mesh grill basket so you can turn them easily and put the sauce in a small pot at the edge of the grill to keep it warm. Grill the shrimp about 3 inches from the fire for about 1½ minutes on each side or until the shrimp just turn pink and feel soft-firm when pressed with your finger. Turn them out onto a serving dish and spoon on enough warm sauce to make them glisten. Sprinkle with parsley and serve with crusty bread, toasted lightly on the grill.

## Lobster Scramble

Anne Johnson of Port Clyde, Maine, contributed this recipe to Bernard Clayton's *Cooking Across America* in her own words. We couldn't improve it, so we're repeating it in the interest of supporting another potential American classic. Good lobster recipes that don't gild the lily are hard to come by. Your seafood market will murder and split the beasts, and don't forget to save the bodies for lobster stock.

As she writes, "It is one of the most delicious ways ever to serve lobster—and so simple. Remove all of the meat from a 1½-pound lobster and cut it into bite-sized pieces. Have the meat at room temperature, of course. In a bowl, stir 4 eggs with a tablespoon of cream or rich milk. Add salt and pepper to taste. Heat butter in a skillet over medium heat. Stir in the lobster pieces and the eggs. Take the skillet off the heat while the eggs are still moist. Lobster and eggs are truly meant for each other." Hey, Anne, how about a pinch of saffron in the butter?

Ms. Johnson touts this for *breakfast*—only in Maine. But lobster scramble would make a showstopper brunch with a basket of warm croissants and brioche. Or a celebratory champagne supper with a dab of caviar on the toast. We're tucking it into our holiday files for Christmas morning.

*Serves 4*

*Give up some freezer space for saving lobster bodies—you won't regret it. Four of them will make a superb stock for soups like cioppino (page 108) and sauces. Cover them with half water and half white wine and add a celery rib, a few peppercorns, a bay leaf, and thyme and parsley sprigs. Fennel seeds are also welcome. Bring to a slow boil and simmer for 1 hour. Strain and reduce by half. Store in small freezer zipper bags. Mark, date, and stack them in your freezer.*

*This is the spot to tout our favorite lobster dish: cold lobster mayonnaise. Bring the lobsters home already steamed and refrigerate them. Enrich 1 cup of Hellmann's or Best Foods mayonnaise by whisking in an egg yolk, 1 tablespoon fresh lemon juice or a couple of drops of pure lemon oil, a teaspoon of Dijon mustard, and salt and freshly ground pepper to taste. Add minced fresh chives, parsley, and tarragon. Crack and dip and have French potato salad (page 41) on the side.*

# Cioppino

Another world-class fish stew, for which we can thank the immigrant Italian fishermen of San Francisco—who either created or preserved it. John Mariani, who wrote the informative *Dictionary of American Food & Drink*, says cioppino comes from the Genoese dialect *cioppin*, which means—guess what?—fish stew. The only thing to remember when selecting the fish is that cioppino is composed predominantly of shellfish, starring either crab or lobster. Besides making the stew base, all you need to do is buy the freshest seafood you can find and afford. And there's the rub. Quality seafood is so pricey now that this formerly frugal workingman's stew has been elevated to a special-occasion dish—and special it is.

*Serves 6*

**The Stock:**

the body and shells of 1 1¼-pound
   steamed lobster, meat reserved
shells from 1 pound (36 to 40)
   medium shrimp, meat reserved
2 8-ounce bottles clam juice
1 cup dry white wine
1 10-ounce can vegetable broth

2 cups water
1 garlic clove, smashed and peeled
   (see page 112)
½ teaspoon dried thyme
1 large bay leaf
8 peppercorns
¼ lemon

**The Cioppino Seasoning Base:**

3 tablespoons olive oil

1½ cups finely chopped onion

1 green bell pepper, cut into ½-inch
 squares

3 garlic cloves, smashed and peeled
 (see page 112)

¼ teaspoon hot red pepper flakes

½ teaspoon saffron threads, crumbled

½ teaspoon salt

1 cup tomato puree

1 14.5-ounce can Muir Glen diced
 tomatoes, undrained

**The Finale:**

18 mussels, scrubbed

1 pound bay scallops, or bass,
 monkfish, snapper, or cod cut into
 bite-sized chunks

the reserved shrimp

the reserved steamed lobster meat,
 chopped

minced flat-leaf parsley for garnish

Put all the stock ingredients in a stainless-steel or enameled stockpot and sim-mer for 45 minutes. Strain and return to the pot. You should have 6 cups stock.

Heat the oil in a medium saucepan and sauté the onion, green pepper, and garlic until soft. Add the red pepper flakes, saffron, and salt. Stir to release flavors. Add the puree and tomatoes and combine this mixture with the fish stock in the soup pot.

Have the stew base hot on the stove. Open the mussels by cooking them in a hot sauté pan over medium-high heat without water. As soon as all the shells are open, transfer them to a bowl to keep warm after straining their liquid into the stew base. Ten minutes before serving, drop any fish chunks into the simmering soup. If you're using all shellfish, 5 minutes will cook everything. Ladle the stew into flat bowls and garnish with the mussels and minced parsley. Serve with sourdough garlic toast.

# Moules Marinière

ow that the mussels you can buy at the market are farmed and no longer subject to the pollution of their natural habitat, perhaps we can go back to one of the
great pleasures of the table without fear of toxicity. Though not as flavorful as the
"wild ones," the farmed mussels are relatively inexpensive and, thankfully, don't require the degree of soaking, scrubbing, and debearding of their vagabond forebears.

*Serves 6*

5 to 6 pounds mussels

6 shallots, minced

1 medium onion, minced

4 garlic cloves, minced

¼ cup extra-virgin olive oil

4 tablespoons (½ stick) butter

pinch of cayenne pepper

½ teaspoon dried thyme or 6 fresh
   sprigs

6 tablespoons minced parsley

3 cups dry white wine

Rinse the mussels and pull off any fuzz. Discard any open ones. In a deep pot,
cook the shallots, onion, and garlic in the olive oil and butter until soft. Add the seasoning and herbs. Add the wine and heat. Add the mussels and bring the liquid to a
simmer. Cook the mussels for 6 to 8 minutes or just until the shells have all opened.
Discard any that don't. Serve them in large, flat-rimmed soup bowls with crusty,
rustic bread to sop up the broth.

*Add ¼ minced fennel bulb to the shallot sauté and a couple of tablespoons
of heavy cream to the broth at the end.*

✐ *California chef Jeremiah Tower adds 3 peeled, seeded, and chopped tomatoes, a couple of bay leaves, and sprigs of tarragon.*

✐ *These mussels make a fine sauce for pasta. Add crisp bits of slab bacon and thicken the sauce with a couple of egg yolks or 1 tablespoon each of butter and flour mixed together. Or just add precooked angel hair pasta to the mussels immediately before serving in time to reheat it.*

✐ BILLI-BI SOUP: *Remove the mussels from their shells, keeping them warm in a covered dish. Strain the liquid in the pot, reduce it over medium-high heat by a third, and add 2 cups heavy cream. Thicken the soup with a* **beurre manié**—*using the back of a fork, mix 4 tablespoons softened butter mixed with 2 tablespoons flour—or, optionally, whisk in 2 egg yolks. Return the mussels to the soup and serve garnished with minced parsley. You'll think you've died and ascended.*

> ## Smashed Garlic
>
> *We often call for garlic to be smashed in this book, which releases the flavorful oil and makes mincing quicker. The way to do this is to put an unpeeled garlic clove on the cutting board and give it a good whack with with your fist on top of the flat side of a chef's knife or smash it with a meat mallet. Bonus: Usually the skin comes off too. Fresh ginger also benefits from this treatment.*
>
> *If peeling garlic drives you nuts, acquire an e-z-roll garlic peeler; you just drop the cloves inside, give it a quick roll, and you're done.*

# Jambalaya

Everyone will tell you that this delicious New Orleans dish, which has become a catchall for leftovers, is just another form of the classic Spanish paella. But according to culinary historian Karen Hess, its real home is Provence, where it was called *jambalaia*. And it's almost exactly the same recipe as pilau, the famous rice dish from the Carolina Low Country. Both pilau and jambalaya were originally made with saffron, and it's worth trying them that way.

At the annual Jambalaya Festival in Gonzales, Louisiana, it's served fiery hot— but try it the way jambalaya connoisseurs like it: a delicate dish made just with shrimp (2 pounds will do it), and with butter instead of bacon fat for sautéing the vegetables. You can always add the hot sauce at the table.

This recipe is a compromise: It's made with smoked sausage and shrimp, but it could also be chicken and ham or duck and oysters. The moderate heat comes from a jalapeño pepper.

*Serves 6*

4 strips of bacon

2 medium white onions, chopped

8 scallions, including the green, chopped

2 garlic cloves, minced

1 medium green bell pepper, chopped

1 jalapeño chile, seeded and finely chopped

1 14.5-ounce can Muir Glen diced tomatoes, undrained, or 4 medium fresh tomatoes, seeded and diced

1 tablespoon tomato paste

1/4 cup chopped parsley

3 cups homemade or canned beef broth

1/8 teaspoon ground cloves

1/8 teaspoon ground allspice

1/2 teaspoon dried thyme leaves

1/4 teaspoon cayenne pepper

salt and freshly ground pepper to taste

2 cups long-grain white rice

1/2 pound smoked beef sausage, chopped and sautéed until brown

1 1/2 pounds (54 to 60) medium shrimp, peeled

In a dutch oven, cook the bacon until golden brown; set aside. Add the onions, scallions, garlic, and sweet and hot peppers to the bacon fat and sauté over medium heat until the vegetables are soft, about 10 minutes.

Add the tomatoes, tomato paste, and parsley and sauté for about 10 minutes, until almost all the liquid is gone. Add the broth, cloves, allspice, thyme, and cayenne pepper; mix well. Add salt and pepper, starting with I tablespoon of salt.

Stir in the rice and sausage, cover the pot tightly, and cook over medium heat for 20 minutes. Fluff the rice with a fork and add the shrimp. Cover and let stand for I0 minutes to cook the shrimp. Serve with the bacon crumbled on top.

# Gumbo

his noble dish from southern Louisiana has both Creoles and Cajuns claiming it as their own—just a sign of what a wonderful dish it is. The word itself comes from a Bantu word for okra, often a key ingredient; gumbo is thickened with either okra or filé, powdered sassafras leaves added just before serving. The classic gumbo is made with a roux, a flavor-stretching and flavor-contributing paste made by stirring flour and fat together over low heat for a long time. (If you want to try it, use ¾ cup oil to 1 cup flour and be careful not to let it burn—stir it from time to time and cook for about 45 minutes. Just a spoonful or two in a soup or stew will contribute a lot of flavor, and you can keep roux on hand in the refrigerator to use as needed.)

This gumbo isn't strictly classic because it doesn't start with roux, it's more soupy than stewish, and it's quick to make. The recipe comes from Jessica Harris (*The Welcome Table*). But it's entirely delicious, a fine introduction to gumbo if you've never had it before. Serve the gumbo in soup plates over a spoonful or two of hot, fluffy rice (we recommend the method used in the shrimp creole recipe on page 104). A not insignificant virtue of this gumbo is that you make it a day ahead of serving; it's also fat free.

5 cups homemade (page 25) or
    canned chicken broth
1 teaspoon dried thyme leaves
2 bay leaves
3 garlic cloves, minced
4 large tomatoes, peeled, seeded, and
    coarsely chopped, or 1 14.5-ounce
    can Muir Glen diced tomatoes,
    undrained
1 teaspoon dried oregano leaves

2 tablespoons grated onion
¾ cup grated celery
1½ pounds (54 to 60) medium
    shrimp, peeled
1 pint shucked fresh oysters
1½ cups crabmeat
1 cup diced cooked chicken
2 teaspoons hot red pepper flakes
1 pound fresh okra, topped, tailed, and
    cut into rounds

Place everything but the okra in a large heavy pot and bring to a boil. Lower the heat and simmer for 10 minutes. Add the okra and continue to simmer over medium heat for 10 minutes (don't let the soup come to a boil again).

Remove the gumbo from the heat and refrigerate it overnight so that the flavors blend. When ready to serve, reheat it, again being careful not to let it boil. Remove the bay leaves and serve hot over rice.

*If fresh okra isn't available, use frozen.*

*If you dislike the gummy quality of cooked okra, just microwave it and add it at the last minute.*

## Maryland Crab Cakes

*J*ust as the Maine lobster has no equal, the Chesapeake Bay blue crab is incomparable and makes superbly delicate crab cakes. To make memorable ones, splurge on exorbitant jumbo lump crabmeat, keep the binder to a minimum, and handle the crab as if it could still pinch. A crab cake that breaks up a little is pardonable. One with a hard crust and a doughy interior is not.

*Serves 4*

1 pound lump crabmeat
1 large egg yolk
2 teaspoons fresh lemon juice
¼ cup mayonnaise, preferably
   Hellmann's or Best Foods

12 to 16 oyster crackers
2 tablespoons minced scallion or
   chives
2 tablespoons minced parsley
cornmeal for coating

**The Sauce:**

½ cup mayonnaise, preferably
  Hellmann's or Best Foods
½ cup sour cream

4 tablespoons (½ stick) butter

1 tablespoon chopped drained large
  capers
Tabasco or other hot sauce to taste

Turn the crabmeat out onto paper towels to drain and carefully pick through it for any cartilage. Don't break up the lumps. Whisk the egg yolk and lemon juice into the mayonnaise. Crush the oyster crackers in a plastic bag with a rolling pin or mallet or reduce them to medium crumbs in a food processor. Toss in the scallion and parsley. Gently fold the mayonnaise into the crabmeat with a rubber spatula, keeping the lumps intact. Fold in most of the cracker crumbs. Test to see if the mixture will hold together, adding more mayonnaise or crumbs if needed. Form the mixture into 8 balls and roll them quickly through the cornmeal for a light coating. Refrigerate for an hour.

For the sauce, mix the mayonnaise and sour cream together, fold in the capers, and spike with Tabasco sauce.

Melt half the butter in each of 2 nonstick skillets that will hold 4 cakes with room between them for easy turning. Sauté the cakes over medium heat, turning only once. Do not attempt to turn them until the first side is well browned and do not press down slightly into patties until they have been turned. Brown the other side and serve with the spicy caper sauce.

# Oyster and Corn Fritters

*O*f all the contemporary fritter batters we tried, this thirty-year-old recipe adapted from *The Horizon Cookbook* is the one we like best for deep frying. Instead of the more common leavened batter most recipes suggest, this one made with beer produces fritters as light as beignets.

*Serves 6*

1 cup flat beer, not light

2 large eggs plus 2 whites

1⅓ cups sifted flour

peanut or corn oil for deep frying

¼ cup minced scallion with 1 inch of
   the green

½ cup fresh or frozen white corn
   kernels, cooked and drained

1 cup shucked fresh oysters, well
   drained and chopped

flour for dusting, preferably Wondra
   instant

¼ teaspoon salt

Whisk together the beer and whole eggs. Gradually beat in the flour. Let stand for 30 minutes. Pour 3 inches of oil in a wok, or fill an electric deep fryer. Heat the oil to 375°. Meanwhile, add the scallion and corn to the batter. Spread the chopped oysters out on a double thickness of paper towels, and blot them lightly. Dust them with flour and fold them into the batter. Beat the egg whites and salt until stiff and fold into the batter. Drop the fritters into the oil by rounded tablespoons and fry until golden. Drain and serve with sauce rémoulade (page 9) or Hellmann's mayonnaise refreshed with a squirt or two of lemon juice and spiked with Tabasco sauce to taste.

## Oyster Stew

A traditional Christmas Eve oyster stew should be enjoyed more often. With a basket of skillet corn bread, you need only a mixed green salad with lemon vinaigrette for a splendid casual company meal. For each serving you need ½ pint shucked oysters, 1 cup half-and-half, a knob of butter, 1 large shallot, minced, freshly ground black pepper, Tabasco sauce to taste, and minced parsley for garnish. Drain the oyster liquor into the half-and-half and bring it to a simmer in a saucepan. Melt the butter in a skillet and cook the shallot until softened. Add the oysters and sauté over high heat, shaking the pan vigorously until the edges of the oysters barely curl. Don't overcook! Season with the pepper and Tabasco. Stir the oysters into the cream base and serve piping hot with a sprinkling of minced parsley.

The cooked fritters will stay crisp in a warm oven for a short time. The batter can be made ahead and kept in the refrigerator if you fold in the beaten egg whites at the last minute.

For clam fritters, simply substitute well-drained clams for the oysters and corn. For crab and corn fritters, use well-picked-over backfin crab for the oysters.

For fresh herb and cheese fritters, delete the oysters and add minced chives, parsley, basil, and Parmesan cheese to the batter. Add a few toasted pine nuts for flavor and texture.

# Spaghetti with Meatballs

As Italians will proudly tell you, there's no such dish in Italy. There's spaghetti, yes, and there are meatballs, but they're not served together. Food writer Nancy Verde Barr, who grew up in an Italian-American family and whose mother's meatball recipe this is, says the two foods were combined in America at the insistence of the government, which thought the Italian diet, so heavy in vegetables, was unhealthy for the digestion (we hadn't yet discovered the healthy Mediterranean diet). So the obliging Italians, so eager to become American, invented this dish, which we all love.

These meatballs have a high proportion of egg, which makes them so tender you don't have to fry them first. The raisins are optional; southern Italians love them in their meatballs.

The meatballs cook right in the meat sauce—use your favorite or a good-quality commercial product.

*Serves 6*

1 pound ground beef

4 large eggs, beaten

1 cup dry bread crumbs

1/4 cup grated pecorino or Parmesan
  cheese, plus cheese for serving
  (optional)

salt and freshly ground pepper
  to taste

1/3 cup dark raisins (optional)

1 quart meat sauce

1 pound imported dried spaghetti

Mix everything but the meat sauce and spaghetti together in a mixing bowl and blend well. With wet hands, roll meatballs any size you like—if you make 36 balls, each diner will have 6 small ones. Drop the meatballs directly into the simmering meat sauce and cook for 30 minutes or until cooked through.

Meanwhile, heat the water for the spaghetti and, when it comes to a boil, add a handful of salt, stir it in, then add the spaghetti. When it's cooked al dente, drain it and mix it with the meat sauce, distributing the meatballs evenly among the diners.

You don't really need extra cheese with this dish, but no doubt you'll be pestered for it, so you might as well put it on the table.

# Pastitsio

Is this an American classic? For Greek-Americans it is, and for those of us fortunate enough to discover it, it quickly became another melting-pot ethnic favorite. Pastitsio is comfort food—moussaka with pasta instead of eggplant. Make double the meat sauce in the moussaka recipe and freeze it for making pastitsio some other time. Meanwhile, look for the authentic noodles in specialty stores. The 10½-inch long, straight, tubular macaroni is available here now, and it's better because the finished dish can be cut into squares like lasagne, which is how the original is commonly served.

*Serves 6 to 8*

1 pound pastitsio noodles, macaroni,
   or ziti
2 tablespoons butter
salt and freshly ground pepper to taste
½ cup grated Parmesan cheese
1 recipe moussaka meat sauce
   (page 76)

6 tablespoons (¾ stick) butter
½ cup flour
3 cups milk, heated
¼ teaspoon freshly grated nutmeg
2 large eggs, lightly beaten

Preheat the oven to 350°. Cook the pasta in a large pot of boiling salted water until al dente, about 10 to 12 minutes. Drain well and butter the noodles. Butter a 9- by 13-inch lasagne pan and put half the noodles on the bottom. Salt and pepper and dust with half the Parmesan. Cover with the meat sauce and add another layer of noodles.

To make the cream sauce, melt the butter in a saucepan and stir in the flour. Cook over low heat, stirring continuously for 2 minutes. Gradually stir in the milk, nutmeg, and salt and pepper to taste. Stir until the sauce thickens. Pour a little of the sauce into the beaten eggs, stir, and return it to the rest. Cover the dish with the sauce and bake for 50 minutes, until the top is set and golden brown. Cut into squares and serve.

# Lasagne

*J*talian-American lasagne, with its rich meat sauce and silken cobwebs of cheese, is mostly a fond memory. The neighborhood family-owned Italian trattoria where Mama did the cooking and the air was heady with the perfume of tomato paste, garlic, olive oil, and oregano has yielded its popularity to more purist Northern Italian–style restaurants. Pity. Although almost every region of Italy has its own style of baking the lasagne noodle, the Southern Italian *Lasagne al Forno* is the most familiar to us, and it isn't difficult or complex to assemble. It's the traditional home-made *ràgu Bolognese* and *besciamella* that takes the time. Our version offers a short-cut or two that don't noticeably diminish the flavor and allow the busiest of us to enjoy this noble dish.

*Serves 6 to 8*

1 pound fresh lasagne sheets, white
 or green

2 tablespoons salt

1 tablespoon olive oil

1 medium onion, minced

2 garlic cloves, minced

1 pound meat loaf mix (beef, pork, and
 veal) or 1 pound ground chuck

salt and freshly ground pepper to taste

½ cup dry red wine

2 cups bottled Italian marinara sauce

½ cup chopped fresh basil leaves

2 cups (1 pound) ricotta cheese

1 egg, beaten

freshly grated nutmeg to taste

½ pound fresh mozzarella, cut into
 small dice

½ cup grated pecorino romano cheese

Cut the lasagne sheets, if necessary, into 5- by 12-inch strips and blanch them in relays in 6 quarts of water brought to a rolling boil with the salt. Drop the strips into the water crisscross fashion so they don't stick together. Cook them for about 3

minutes or until the pasta is slightly undercooked. Spread the cooked strips out on a cookie sheet and lightly blot up any little pools of water with a paper towel. Oil or butter the bottom of a 9- by 13-inch lasagne pan and line it with a single layer of pasta strips. Do not overlap them but do let the strips climb the sides and ends of the pan a little to keep the sauce from oozing out.

Pour the oil into a heavy skillet and sauté the onion and garlic until the onion is transluscent, not brown. Add the ground meat and cook over medium-high heat, breaking up the lumps with the back of a wooden spoon. When the meat is cooked and smooth, season with salt and pepper, add the red wine, and sizzle off the alcohol for a minute. Reduce the heat to low, add the marinara sauce and basil, and simmer for 15 minutes.

Mix together the ricotta, the beaten egg, nutmeg, and mozzarella and romano cheeses. Lightly salt it and add freshly ground pepper.

Preheat the oven to 375°.

To assemble the dish, spread a thin layer of meat sauce over the pasta lining the pan. Spread a thin layer of the cheese and egg mixture over the meat sauce and top with another layer of lasagne strips. Repeat this layering sequence using all the lasagne and resisting the temptation to thicken the sauce layers. The final layer should be cheese. Bake for 40 minutes. Check after 20 minutes should an excess of watery juice need to be poured off.

> ➣ Lasagne reheats perfectly, in fact benefits from it. You can complete the dish in the morning and reheat it for dinner or cover and refrigerate it for a couple of days. You can also freeze it, so consider making two while you're at it— one to serve, one to freeze.

> ➣ Baked pasta invites variations. If you don't want to fool with lasagne sheets, try layering precooked spaghetti. Consider using green lasagne noodles (made with spinach).

➣ Make a "meat" sauce of sautéed greens such as chard, spinach, mustard greens, or arugula; mixed or not. Season them with minced garlic and onion and add in sliced and sautéed cremini or portobello mushrooms. Layer the greens with the ricotta cheese mixture or simply mix ricotta with enough sour cream to smooth it and spread a thick layer in the middle and on top. Dust generously with grated Parmesan cheese.

➣ There are both imported and domestic "instant" lasagne sheets on the market that require no precooking. Look for them in your specialty food store.

➣ If you own perforated baking sheets, they're perfect for cooling and draining the precooked lasagne.

➣ Undoubtedly, homemade pasta is the best because you can roll the sheets as thin as parchment and use multiple layers, producing a more authentic lasagne. If you have a pasta machine languishing in a bottom cabinet, you can use it to roll out commercial fresh pasta thinner.

# Spaghetti with Clam Sauce

*O*ne spur-of-the-moment pasta dish most of us think of preparing when we run out of time and creativity is spaghetti with clam sauce. The clam sauce is usually hastily assembled using canned clams, and although satisfying, it's a pale shadow of the original, made with very small twin-necked clams found off Italian shores. Our own American cherrystones or littlenecks make an admirable pasta sauce, so when you can find them and they aren't too dear, try this dish without using the can opener. Instead of spaghetti or linguine, we're using thin strands of pasta.

*Serves 4*

2 dozen cherrystone or littleneck
 clams, scrubbed
¼ cup extra-virgin olive oil
3 garlic cloves, minced
2 tablespoons chopped flat-leaf
 parsley
1 tablespoon chopped fresh oregano
 or 1 teaspoon dried

4 canned Italian plum tomatoes,
 drained and torn into strips, or
 1 cup Muir Glen canned diced,
 drained
pinch of hot red pepper flakes
salt and freshly ground pepper to taste
½ cup dry white wine
1 pound imported dried spaghettini or
 angel hair pasta
2 tablespoons chopped fresh basil
 leaves

Scrub the clams in the sink in cold water, discarding broken or open ones. Put the clams in a soup pot. Cover and cook over high heat, shaking the pot often. Remove the clams to a bowl as they open fully, which should take about 5 minutes. Remove the clams from their shells, straining the liquid from the pan and bowl into a measuring cup. Chop the clams, coat them with some of the olive oil, and set aside. Pour the rest of the oil into a skillet, add the garlic and herbs, and sauté until the garlic softens. Add the tomatoes, red pepper flakes, salt, pepper, wine, and strained clam broth. Simmer the sauce for about 10 minutes, reducing the liquid slightly.

Meanwhile, bring a large pot of water to a boil over high heat. Add the pasta and cook until al dente, about 6 to 8 minutes. Add the drained pasta, clams, and basil to the skillet and toss well. Serve immediately in heated flat-rimmed soup bowls.

*If you're using canned clams, you'll need three 6½-ounce cans of chopped clams or two 10-ounce cans of whole baby clams.*

# Spaghetti alla Carbonara

*T*his is the addictive dish that writer Calvin Trillin thinks should be substituted for turkey at Thanksgiving. We could live with that.

In the bad old days of Italian cooking in America, we had to use boiled bacon for this dish, which in Italy is made with guanciale, cured pork cheek, or pancetta (pronounced pan-CHET-uh), the cured unsmoked bacon that is now widely available in America, even sometimes at the supermarket. If you get your hands on some guanciale, which is unlikely, make this dish with it. Otherwise, it's worth searching out pancetta since it keeps almost forever in the freezer and is very useful for making soups, sauces, and stews. Besides, if you have it on hand, you can whip up this pasta at a moment's notice from kitchen staples.

*Serves 4*

salt

12 ounces dried spaghetti

4 ounces pancetta, chopped

4 large egg yolks

¼ cup freshly grated pecorino cheese
   (Italian sheep cheese)

¼ cup freshly grated Parmesan
   cheese

additional grated Parmesan and
   pecorino cheese for serving

Put a large pot of water on to boil for the spaghetti. When the pot is boiling, add a handful of salt and stir it into the water. Put the spaghetti into the pot and cook until it's al dente, about 8 minutes.

Meanwhile, fry the pancetta in a large skillet just until it starts to brown. In a bowl, beat together the egg yolks and half the cheese.

When the pasta is ready, drain it and put it in the skillet with the pancetta over low heat, mixing rapidly. Add the eggs and cheese and the remaining cheese, turn off the heat, mix well, and serve at once. Pass bowls of extra Parmesan and pecorino at the table and pass a pepper grinder as well.

*If pancetta isn't available, you can use diced slab bacon. Drop it into a pot of boiling water for a couple of minutes to correct the saltiness, and cook it longer than the pancetta, until it's golden brown.*

# Macaroni and Cheese

This is the easiest version we've found, and it tastes very good. It isn't quite as creamy as the classic version, which is made with a white sauce—check the notes at the end of the recipe if you want to spring for the extra work. The classic version is all Cheddar, of course, but we love it with mixed cheeses too.

*Serves 4*

½ pound elbow macaroni

1 tablespoon butter

1 large egg, beaten

freshly ground pepper to taste

1 teaspoon salt

1 to 1½ teaspoons dry mustard, preferably Colman's, to taste

1 tablespoon hot water

3 cups grated sharp Cheddar cheese

1 cup milk

Preheat the oven to 350°.

Boil the macaroni in salted water until just tender, according to the package directions. Drain thoroughly and put the macaroni in a large mixing bowl. Stir in the butter and egg along with some pepper. Mix the salt and mustard with the hot water and stir into the macaroni. Add the cheese, holding back enough to sprinkle over the top.

Put the macaroni and cheese into a buttered casserole, sprinkle the reserved cheese over the top, and pour the milk over everything. Bake for 45 minutes or until the top is crusty.

➤ We like this dish made with the sharpest Cheddar we can find, which is usually Canadian white extra-sharp. The yellow cheese looks cheerful, but it's artificially colored.

➤ You may want even more mustard; try 2 teaspoons.

➤ CREAMY MACARONI WITH THREE CHEESES: *Try using a thicker noodle, such as penne rigate or small ziti. For a pound of pasta, use 2 cups grated Cheddar, a thin wedge of Roquefort, and 1 cup grated Parmesan. Cook the pasta and toss with 1 tablespoon butter. Make a white sauce: In a saucepan over medium-low heat, melt 2 tablespoons butter. When the butter is foaming, stir in 2 tablespoons flour until mixed. Let the mixture cook for a couple of minutes, then add 2 cups warm milk and whisk into a sauce. Add a little dry mustard, a shake of cayenne, and salt and pepper to taste. Add the cheeses, stir until they're melted, and pour the sauce over the pasta before putting it in the casserole. Top with buttered bread crumbs and bake as directed above.*

➤ Sometimes sharp aged Cheddar gets grainy and curdles when it's cooked. It still tastes delicious, but you can avoid the problem by mixing in some fontina, Swiss, or Monterey Jack cheese.

# Welsh Rarebit

*A*lmost nothing tastes better for supper on a cold winter's eve than a cup of homemade vegetable soup and a creamy cheese rarebit. Such recipes are never quite committed to memory if they aren't a frequent choice—unless, of course, you live in New England, where rarebit is standard in every good cook's repertoire. We like this version because of its complex flavors, and it looks as appetizing as it tastes.

*Serves 4*

3 tablespoons butter

4 cups grated aged sharp Cheddar
    cheese

½ cup ale or dark beer

1 teaspoon Worcestershire sauce

1 teaspoon dry mustard, preferably
    Colman's

½ teaspoon paprika

¼ teaspoon cayenne pepper

¼ teaspoon salt

2 large eggs, lightly beaten

8 slices of firm bakery white bread,
    crustless, toasted and cut into
    triangles

Melt the butter in a heavy saucepan over moderate heat until it sizzles. Add the cheese and all the other ingredients except the eggs and bread, stirring continuously until the cheese melts and the mixture is smooth. Remove the pan from the heat and beat in the eggs, then return it to a low heat and stir until the rarebit has thickened. Immediately pour the hot cheese over the toast points.

# Side Dishes

# Saratoga Chips

*What?* Make your own potato chips? No, we aren't mad—we just know a good thing when we rediscover it. The original thin potato chip was given away as a bar snack at Moon's Lake Lodge in Saratoga, New York, in the mid-nineteenth century and started a zillion-dollar American industry that is still trying to duplicate them. The fact is that you can't buy a chip as thin and ethereal as you can make at home—they'd never ship. So, for a real treat for your family and friends, make a batch or two and pray they don't get devoured before you can store some in a tight tin. You will need one of those inexpensive plastic V slicers or a French mandoline as well as a suitable pot for deep frying. A wok or electric frying pan is fine if you don't have an electric kettle fryer. Too much trouble? Wait till you taste them.

twice as many all-purpose potatoes as
   you think you'll slice—don't use
   baking or new potatoes

peanut oil for deep frying
salt

Peel the potatoes. Lay paper towels on your countertop and slice the potatoes right over them, spreading the slices out to blot dry as you go. With a good slicer, you can go through half a dozen potatoes in no time. The slices should be just a tad thicker than paper-thin. If they're too flexible and transparent, they'll end up with an unbalanced proportion of fat to potato. Test-cook a few before you finish slicing. The oil should be pristine and the temperature at 375°. Cooking the potato is just a matter of dropping a few dry slices at a time into the fat and waiting a moment until they shade beautifully from white to golden brown. Remove with a slotted spoon and drain on paper towels. Salt to taste.

   *Soaking the potatoes in ice water doesn't affect the result, but the benefits of soaking may have something to do with the age of the potato and the amount*

# Side Dishes

# Saratoga Chips

*What?* Make your own potato chips? No, we aren't mad—we just know a good thing when we rediscover it. The original thin potato chip was given away as a bar snack at Moon's Lake Lodge in Saratoga, New York, in the mid–nineteenth century and started a zillion-dollar American industry that is still trying to duplicate them. The fact is that you can't buy a chip as thin and ethereal as you can make at home—they'd never ship. So, for a real treat for your family and friends, make a batch or two and pray they don't get devoured before you can store some in a tight tin. You will need one of those inexpensive plastic V slicers or a French mandoline as well as a suitable pot for deep frying. A wok or electric frying pan is fine if you don't have an electric kettle fryer. Too much trouble? Wait till you taste them.

*twice as many all-purpose potatoes as*        *peanut oil for deep frying*
*you think you'll slice—don't use*        *salt*
*baking or new potatoes*

Peel the potatoes. Lay paper towels on your countertop and slice the potatoes right over them, spreading the slices out to blot dry as you go. With a good slicer, you can go through half a dozen potatoes in no time. The slices should be just a tad thicker than paper-thin. If they're too flexible and transparent, they'll end up with an unbalanced proportion of fat to potato. Test-cook a few before you finish slicing. The oil should be pristine and the temperature at 375°. Cooking the potato is just a matter of dropping a few dry slices at a time into the fat and waiting a moment until they shade beautifully from white to golden brown. Remove with a slotted spoon and drain on paper towels. Salt to taste.

*Soaking the potatoes in ice water doesn't affect the result, but the benefits of soaking may have something to do with the age of the potato and the amount of starch. If your test doesn't give you the best chip you ever tasted, try soaking the rest of the slices for an hour or so. Be sure to drain them well and blot dry.*

*It's admittedly un-American, but the most divine homemade chip of all is fried in half peanut oil and half olive oil—or all olive oil. The subtle flavor the olive oil adds is memorable and deliciously reminiscent of those sublime chips one finds in Spain and Portugal. Try it.*

*We often don't bother to peel the potatoes, but they don't look as glorious.*

## Mashed Potatoes

If you had no other culinary achievements, making great mashed potatoes could assure your reputation as a cook—so beloved are these simple spuds. And so dreadful are the botched versions: watery, gluey, lumpy, tasteless.

Your object is to have dry, fluffy potatoes enriched with something delicious like butter, cream, and milk. Low-fat perpetrators can use buttermilk, which makes wonderful mashed potatoes. The tricks lie in using the right potatoes, drying them out, and using the right tools to mash them. But read on.

*Serves 8*

8 large Idaho or russet potatoes or 12 Yukon Golds, peeled and halved

salt to taste

1½ cups cream, half-and-half, or buttermilk

freshly ground pepper to taste

butter to taste

Preheat the oven to 325°. In a large saucepan, cover the potatoes with cold water and set over medium heat. When the water comes to a boil, add salt to taste and gently boil the potatoes, partially covered, for 20 minutes. Check for doneness with a fork; they should be tender but not mushy. When they're done, drain them and put them on a baking sheet to dry out in the oven (this also gives you a little extra time to attend to other last-minute kitchen jobs).

When you're just about ready to serve the potatoes, have the cream or butter-milk warm, but don't let the buttermilk simmer, or it will separate. Put the potatoes through a potato ricer or a food mill directly back into the cooking pot. Set the pot over low heat. Gradually add the liquid while beating the potatoes vigorously with a wooden spoon. Once you have the right consistency, add salt and pepper and as much butter as you dare. Pile the potatoes in a warm serving dish, plop a big chunk of but-ter on top, and serve immediately.

STEAMED POTATOES: *You can save time and maybe even trouble by cut-ting the potatoes into small pieces and steaming them. In that case you can add half a head of peeled garlic cloves to the steaming basket and mash them right in with the potatoes.*

---

*Hash Browns*

*Karen Gantz Zahler reports in* The Taste of New York *that the famous New York Palm Restaurant, where they make the best hash browns to pass your lips, presses undercooked new potatoes through a wide metal strainer, dis-carding the skins that stick to the mesh. The squashed potatoes are then fried for 10 minutes in very hot clarified butter, which resists burning at high tem-peratures. Flip and brown the potatoes on both sides and sprinkle liberally with salt and freshly ground black pepper. (To clarify butter, melt it in the mi-crowave and leave it to cool. Skim off the pure fat and discard the solids and water.)*

*⤳ BAKED POTATOES: Instead of drying the potatoes in the oven, try baking them in their skins to begin with, in a 375° oven for up to 1½ hours or until they're entirely soft. Cut them in half horizontally, scoop out the interior, and proceed with the recipe. You can bake a little garlic while you're at it—wrap it in foil and take it out of the oven after 45 minutes.*

## Potato Pancakes

*L*ace-edged and glossy brown with a pebbly, creamy interior, potato pancakes with applesauce and juicy link sausage, or ribs and sauerkraut, are just plain old-fashioned wonderful. They even make a dandy supper on their own. There's nothing either mysterious or difficult about making good potato pancakes, but, like all pancakes, they don't wait very patiently. If you want to make them for a crowd, see the tip at the end of the recipe notes.

### *Makes 16 to 18 pancakes*

*2 large Idaho or russet potatoes, about*
    *1¼ pounds peeled*
*½ cup grated or minced onion*
*salt and freshly ground pepper to taste*

*2 tablespoons flour*
*2 large eggs*
*1 tablespoon cream or milk*
*6 to 8 tablespoons butter*

Stand a box grater in a large bowl and grate the potatoes on the largest hole or use the grating disk (not the steel blade) of your food processor. Add the onion and, with a double sheet of paper towel over the mixture, press it against the side of the bowl, draining off the water. Sprinkle with salt, pepper, and flour.

In a small bowl, whisk the eggs with the cream and toss to coat the potatoes. Melt about 1½ tablespoons of the butter in a 10-inch nonstick skillet, covering the bottom generously. With your fingertips, scoop enough of the mixture into the pan to make thin pancakes about 2½ inches in diameter, leaving just enough space between to ease the turning. Cook over medium-high heat until the lacy edges and the bottom are brown, then flip them over. It will take about 8 minutes per batch. Butter the pan for each round, keeping the cooked pancakes warm on a paper towel–lined cookie sheet in a very low oven. Working with 2 pans at once is quicker. Serve the pancakes with applesauce.

➥ *Superb with thin slices of gravlax (page 4), a large dot of sour cream, and a shower of snipped chives.*

➥ *Jewish latkes are made the same way but are classically cooked in rendered chicken fat.*

➥ *For breakfast, make them with half sweet potatoes and a grating of fresh nutmeg. Serve with warm maple syrup and a side of crispy bacon.*

➥ *If you're making potato pancakes for a crowd, try this trick from California cook Diane Worthington: Overlap the cooled cooked pancakes on sheets of aluminum foil, cover with top sheets, and crimp the edges to seal. Freeze the flat packets. When you're ready to serve, preheat the oven to 425° and place the packets on a baking sheet. Remove the top sheet and bake for 5 to 7 minutes, until the pancakes are hot and crisp.*

# Grits

*O*nce considered nothing more than a staple of white trash cooking, grits have become amazingly chic—probably because polenta is so trendy, and after all, both of them are just ground corn. We're not talking about the bland, mushy industrial-quality grits found in most supermarkets, which are actually ground hominy, corn that's lost its hull and germ in the course of being cured in lye. The best grits are stone-ground or water-ground and have the germ intact. Look for speckled heart grits, which sometimes turn up in the supermarket.

The longer you cook the grits, and the more butter you add, the better they'll be. We think they're best of all—and easiest—cooked all day long in an electric slow cooker. But half-hour grits are fine; you just have to give them an occasional stir.

*Serves 6*

1 quart water

4 tablespoons (½ stick) butter or more
   to taste

salt to taste

1 cup stone-ground or water-ground
   whole-grain grits

In a large heavy pot such as a dutch oven, bring the water, butter, and salt to a boil. Add the grits in a gradual stream. Bring the pot back to a boil, then reduce the heat to simmer. Cook, uncovered, at a steady simmer, stirring from time to time so they don't stick. They'll be done after about 25 minutes, but taste them to be sure they're ready. If you want to cook them longer, you may have to add more water. And of course you can add more butter at any point.

Once the grits are cooked, taste for salt, cover the pot, and turn the heat down to the lowest setting to keep them warm for a few minutes.

*The grits become naturally creamy, but you can intensify the creaminess by adding milk or even cream as they cook.*

❧ *If you're using the slow-cooker method, check the liquid level every now and then—you may need to add more if the grits are looking dry. They should be soupy.*

❧ *It's easy to oversalt the grits; hold back until they're ready to be sure you really need salt.*

❧ *You can add a minced jalapeño pepper, minced garlic, grated cheese, bits of ham, or anything else you might think of putting in polenta if you're serving the grits as a side dish. For breakfast, it's best to keep it simple and just use the butter.*

❧ *To make grits cakes, chill the cooked grits and form them into little cakes. Dust them with flour or cornmeal and fry them in melted butter until golden brown.*

❧ *If you're living outside the Grits Belt and you're eager to try good grits, you can mail-order them from Hoppin' John's at (803) 577-6404 or Callaway Gardens at (404) 663-5100.*

## Spoon Bread

Outside the South and the Midwest spoon bread isn't on many tables, which is a pity. Lots of people think it's a bread, which it isn't; it's actually a very delicate dish, a cross between a soufflé (but you don't have to beat the egg whites) and a pudding that makes a great side dish. Lots of butter on top is the rule. Spoon bread is also great on its own for Sunday supper or for breakfast—try it with molasses or maple syrup. Like all soufflés, spoon bread will fall quickly, so serve it right out of the oven.

*Serves 6*

2 cups water

1 teaspoon salt

¾ cup cornmeal, yellow or white, preferably water-ground or stone-ground

4 tablespoons (½ stick) butter at room temperature

4 large eggs, beaten

1 cup buttermilk mixed with a pinch of baking soda

Preheat the oven to 400°. Butter a 2-quart soufflé dish.

In a medium saucepan over medium heat, bring the water to a boil. Add the salt and cornmeal in a steady stream and cook, stirring, for about a minute, until thickened. Beat in the remaining ingredients until smooth, then pour the mixture into the soufflé dish. Bake for about 40 minutes or until a tester inserted in the center comes out dry. Serve immediately.

*Spoon bread batter also makes delicious griddle cakes. Drop the batter by spoonfuls onto a hot buttered griddle and turn them when the edges begin to look dry.*

*You can add lots of interesting things to spoon bread, from a little grated Parmesan and/or bits of ham or crisp bacon to snipped chives to kernels of corn to dice of red pepper or jalapeño—but sauté the peppers first in butter for a few minutes.*

# Polenta
# (aka Cornmeal Mush)

*E*ven a lot of professional cooks think that polenta is a different thing from cornmeal, but it isn't—and cornmeal mush is the same thing as the Italian dish, though not cooked so long and not regarded with such reverence as its Italian cousin.

Traditional polenta requires a good 45 minutes of fairly constant stirring, so it's not in the no-fuss category. Of course there's instant polenta, which is a useful product, especially for making firm polenta to grill. Instant polenta is usually made from inferior corn, so you're sacrificing a little taste and texture for convenience—still, better instant polenta than no polenta at all.

But here are two other solutions to the problem: *New York Times* food writer Suzanne Hamlin's oven method—which requires no stirring, just an hour in the oven—and the microwave method. You don't have to worry about getting lumps either way because you mix the cornmeal with the water to begin with. Both these methods will produce creamy, intensely corn-tasting polenta. To make firm polenta, see the notes below.

The key to any polenta is to use the best, freshest cornmeal you can get your hands on: medium-textured or coarse or a mix; stone-ground; white or yellow. One reliable brand with national distribution is Goya. Cornmeal is extremely perishable; keep it in the refrigerator.

### For the Oven Method (Serves 6 to 8):

1 quart cold water or broth

1 cup cornmeal

1 teaspoon salt

¼ pound (1 stick) butter

grated Parmesan cheese (optional)

## Oven Method:

Preheat the oven to 350°. Whisk the water with the cornmeal and salt until smooth. Pour the mixture into a 9- by 12- by 2-inch roasting pan or other large metal pan, cover securely with foil, and bake for 1 hour. You can stir the polenta a couple of times, but you don't have to.

At the end of the hour, take the polenta out of the oven, remove the foil, and check for doneness—if it's very soupy, return it to the oven for a few minutes. Vigorously stir in the butter. The polenta will hold, covered with the foil, for an hour in a 250° oven.

## For the Microwave Method (Serves 4):

½ cup cornmeal

2½ cups water or broth

½ teaspoon salt

4 tablespoons (½ stick) butter
  (optional)

grated Parmesan cheese to taste
  (optional)

## Microwave Method:

Combine the cornmeal with the broth and salt. Cook, uncovered, on HIGH for 6 minutes. Remove and stir, cover, and cook for 6 minutes more, until the polenta is thick. Let stand for a few minutes, then stir in butter and cheese if you like and serve.

➤ *To make firm polenta, pour the cooked mush into a Pyrex loaf pan and let it set in the refrigerator. It will keep for up to a week in the refrigerator if you don't add butter and cheese. Slice the firm polenta and fry, grill, or broil it. Serve topped with sautéed wild mushrooms with thyme or mixed fried peppers or a simple fresh chunky tomato sauce.*

➤ *Coarsely ground cornmeal will take longer to cook and will require more liquid. If the polenta is getting too thick, just add more liquid.*

# Red Beans and Rice

The late great Louis Armstrong was perhaps America's greatest fan of this legendary Creole dish—he signed his letters, "Red Beans and Ricely Yours." In New Orleans, red beans and rice were traditionally served on Monday, which was also laundry day. Lucille Armstrong insisted that the rice shouldn't be mixed with the beans but served separately, but of course you can do as you please.

The rice is cooked in the typical Creole way, which gives it a light, fluffy, every-grain-standing-separate quality.

### The Beans:

1 pound dried red kidney beans, soaked overnight in water to cover

1 ham bone with some meat still attached or 2 ham hocks or 1 pound smoked sausage

1 large onion, finely chopped

½ green bell pepper, finely chopped

2 garlic cloves, finely chopped

1 bay leaf

salt, freshly ground pepper, and hot red pepper flakes to taste

### The Rice:

6 cups water

2 teaspoons salt

1 tablespoon olive oil

2 cups long-grain white rice

Put the soaked beans along with the soaking water in a large heavy pot—a dutch oven is perfect. Add the remaining beans ingredients. Add water to cover if necessary and set the pot over low heat, covered, for about 3 hours or until the beans have a stewlike consistency. (Actually, there are two schools of thought here; you can also take the beans off the fire after they're just tender, in about 30 minutes.) Taste for seasoning and adjust. Take the meat off the bones and finely chop; return it to the pot. Fish out the bay leaf and serve the beans in soup plates, with the rice on the side or the rice mixed in with the beans, as you prefer.

For the rice, bring the water to a boil in a large saucepan. Add the salt and the olive oil, then slowly add the rice. Keep boiling the rice, uncovered, until it's soft, about 15 minutes. Drain it in either a strainer or a colander. You can put the strainer with the rice back into the pot to steam over a couple of cups of hot water; cover it closely. Or put the rice in the colander in the oven—325° is about right—for 10 or 15 minutes to dry out and plump up.

✍ *Some recipes call for pepperoni slices in this mélange.*

✍ *Some people like a lot of fire in this dish—for them, have a little bottle of hot sauce on the table.*

---

✍

*Scalloped Potatoes*

*Thinly slice as many peeled potatoes as the number of servings you want to make and one onion for every six servings. Make a single overlapping layer of potatoes in the bottom of a buttered shallow casserole and add a couple of separated onion slices. Salt and pepper it, dot with butter bits, and dust lightly with a little flour shaken from a small strainer. Continue layering, seasoning, buttering, and flouring. Pour in enough milk to cover the potatoes and bake the casserole in a 350° oven for an hour.*

---

# Risotto

At first we thought we'd put risotto in the main-dish chapter because who, we reasoned, would be willing to stand at the range, wooden spoon in a frozen grip, slowly stirring rice for 30 minutes? Certainly not a busy cook. As risotto lovers, we've always respected the time-honored cooking mystique but decided to try a more cavalier approach. It turns out the trick isn't in the constant stirring but just in watching and tasting. This is our favorite risotto, which takes 30 minutes start to finish, leaving hands free to assemble the rest of a simple and simply delicious meal.

*Serves 4*

2 tablespoons extra-virgin olive oil

1 garlic clove, minced

2 shallots, minced

2½ cups homemade or condensed
    canned (undiluted) beef broth

½ cup full-bodied red wine

1 cup Arborio rice

1 teaspoon salt

2 tablespoons butter

Parmesan cheese to taste

Heat the olive oil in a heavy saucepan and sauté the garlic and shallots until they're softened. Meanwhile, bring the broth and wine to a fast simmer on an adjacent burner. Add the rice to the oil and stir well until all the grains are coated and the rice becomes translucent. Drizzle in about ¼ cup of the broth, stirring the rice well until the visible liquid is absorbed but the rice still looks moist and creamy, which is the way the risotto should look until it's done. Repeat once more. Then pour in about a third of the remaining broth, stir well, and leave it simmering gently over low heat. Check and stir in about 10 minutes, adding the rest of the broth. In the last 10 minutes the risotto will absorb the liquid quickly. It will be done when the kernels are soft, with just a little bite at the center. It will be creamy and moist, but there will be no liquid in the bottom of the pan when you stir down to it. If you need a tablespoon or two more liquid, add water. At the end, add the butter and stir the risotto rapidly to incorporate. Instead of folding in grated Parmesan—and this may seem like heresy—add thin shavings with a vegetable peeler to the top of each serving, or pass the grated cheese separately; stirring it in tends to make the risotto sticky and dry.

    *Adding red wine gives the risotto a robust flavor, but you can use all broth—in which case add a pinch of saffron threads to the garlic and shallots and you'll have risotto Milanese.*

    *Adding sautéed mushrooms to risotto is a natural. Equally good is slant-cut grilled asparagus.*

    *Serve risotto with ossobuco alla gremolata (page 88), scampi alla griglia (page 105), or a roast chicken (page 96).*

## Boston Baked Beans

Baked beans are not just a New England tradition; they're a ritual. It's that ritual that makes this Puritan bean dish taste so special. Unlike most regional recipes, there's little argument about how to make them. Perhaps that's because busy Puritan housewives had them baked in their own bean pots by the same community baker each Saturday when the Sabbath started at sundown. We're willing to concede that one shouldn't be tempted to doctor up canned beans and pass them off as authentic. A few things should remain sacred.

    This recipe will feed a 12-man platoon generously, but it neatly fills a standard 3-quart bean pot, and if you're going to keep the oven going for three or four hours, you might as well tuck a quart or so of those beans in the freezer. We urge you to search out a proper glazed earthenware lidded bean pot with the all-important narrow neck. The weight and bulbous shape contribute greatly to the silken quality of the beans, and you'll find many other uses for it.

*Serves 12 or more*

2 pounds dried pea or navy beans
½ pound lean salt pork
2 small onions, peeled and quartered
½ cup dark unsulphured molasses
½ cup packed dark brown sugar or
    pure maple syrup

¼ cup tomato paste (optional)
2 tablespoons dry mustard, preferably
    Colman's
2 teaspoons freshly ground black
    pepper
1 quart boiling water

Put the beans in a colander, pick through them for pebbles and debris. Rinse and cover with cold water in the bean pot. Let them soak overnight. Drain the soaked beans in a colander and rinse. When you're ready to bake the beans, preheat the oven to 225°. Cut 3 thin slices from the salt pork and set aside for the top of the pot. Leaving the rind intact, cut the rest into 1-inch-thick slices and then cut each of those down to the rind in 1-inch segments. Put 2 of these strips of connected squares in the bottom of the pot along with 4 onion quarters. Fill the pot half full of beans. Repeat the pork and onion. Pour in the rest of the beans. Mix the rest of the ingredients into the boiling water, stirring until everything dissolves. Pour over the beans and fill the pot with enough additional water to cover. Put the reserved salt pork strips on top.

Put the lid in place and bake, adding more water as needed to keep the beans covered. Start checking the water level after about 2 hours. After 3 hours, spoon out a few beans and begin testing for tenderness. Adjust the seasoning if needed. Cooking times for beans are unpredictable, so test for doneness by tasting and by blowing hard on a spoonful. If the skins fly off, the beans are done, which can take from 3 to 5 hours. Bake uncovered for the last hour.

    *Don't be concerned if the beans are tender, but very soupy. They will absorb the liquid as they stand, and become creamy. You'll probably even have to add more water when you reheat them.*

🖝 Boston beans should be only moderately sweet. Resist adding more sweeteners than called for since the sweetness intensifies as the cooking liquid is absorbed.

🖝 Additional salt will probably be needed but should be stirred into the pot after the beans are done.

🖝 We like to suspend a whole head of garlic from a long piece of cooking twine to the very bottom of the bean pot. It not only adds a very subtle flavor to the beans, but the roasted garlic squeezed from the cloves when you cut them is luscious.

🖝 A real bean pot—as well as interesting heirloom beans to go in it—can be mail-ordered from La Cuisine (800) 521-1176.

---

🖝

## *Fried Onion Rings*

*This is as good as they get: Dump ½ cup flour and ¼ cup cornmeal into a deep bowl with a pinch of cayenne pepper or chili powder. Add enough beer to smooth the batter—not too thin, not too thick, but just right to coat the thickly sliced rings. Drop them into deep 375° oil until they're golden and crispy. Drain on paper towels, salt, and serve hot.*

# Fried Green Tomatoes

whole new generation has fallen in love with fried green tomatoes. The only hard part is finding them—tomato gardeners and farmers' markets are great sources, and in the fall, just before the first frost, you can find green tomatoes almost everywhere. Although picked-ripe red tomatoes are more and more available, a number of grocers still have boxes of green tomatoes waiting to ripen in a back room—it's worth asking.

*Serves 4*

4 hard green tomatoes, sliced about ¼ inch thick

buttermilk for dipping the slices

cornmeal for dredging the slices

salt and freshly ground pepper to taste

bacon fat for panfrying

Have ready a large skillet, preferably cast iron. Set out a little assembly line: the sliced tomatoes, a bowl of buttermilk, the cornmeal seasoned with salt and pepper.

Heat a couple of tablespoons of bacon fat over high heat in the skillet. When it's very hot but not smoking, dip the tomato slices first in the buttermilk, then in the seasoned cornmeal, and drop them into the skillet without crowding. Sauté them, uncovered, for about 5 minutes; when they're golden brown, turn them over and fry for another 5 minutes—they should be crisp outside and soft inside. Serve immediately.

*Bacon fat is the classic cooking medium, but if you'd rather not use it, try olive oil, which will still produce a crispy fried tomato, with a somewhat more exotic flavor.*

# Fried Apples

**F**ried apples are a delicious, nearly forgotten dish that need a movie to make them as eroticized as fried green tomatoes. Fried apples are even easier to make, and they're delicious for breakfast with sausage or ham or bacon, alongside waffles, or for dinner with ham or roast pork. You might think they wouldn't be very good with Italian sausage, but they are.

*Serves 6*

2 tablespoons butter

4 tart, unpeeled green apples, thinly
   sliced

sugar to taste

sprinkling of freshly grated nutmeg or
   ground cinnamon (optional)

In a large skillet, melt the butter over medium-high heat. When it's bubbling, add the apple slices and sprinkle with a spoonful or two of sugar and the spices if desired. With a spatula, turn the slices over and over until they're golden brown and the sugar has caramelized.

➤ *Try frying the apples in bacon fat.*

➤ *Crowned with a scoop of vanilla ice cream, these can also be dessert.*

➤ *You can make apple rings, which are pretty and just a little more fuss—core the apples and slice them a little thicker, which means you cook them a little longer.*

# Corn Pudding

e can't seem to find a better recipe for this dish than legendary Southern cook Camille Glenn's, which we also used in our first book, *Great Food Without Fuss*. But it's for sure a classic, it's the best and easiest, and you need to have it, so here it is.

This recipe is best made with fresh summer corn, but it also works with frozen corn kernels.

*Serves 6*

6 ears of tender fresh corn

3 large eggs, beaten

1 cup heavy cream

⅓ cup milk

1 teaspoon salt

1 tablespoon sugar

Preheat the oven to 350°. To get the corn off the cob, stand an ear of corn on its large end inside a bowl and cut down the rows of kernels as close to the cob as you can, letting the kernels fall into the bowl. Scrape the cob well to extract all the juice.

Mix the remaining ingredients in a large bowl and add the corn. Pour the mixture into a buttered shallow 1½-quart glass baking dish or casserole. Place in a roasting pan or other shallow pan in the oven and add warm water to come halfway up the dish. Bake for 1 hour or until a knife inserted in the middle comes out clean.

*To use frozen corn, mix 2 cups with ¼ cup milk in a food processor.*

## Rice Pilaf

*For 3 cups cooked (1 cup raw) long-grain rice to serve 4 to 6 people, sauté ½ cup minced onion or shallot in 3 tablespoons butter, or half oil and half butter, until softened. Add 1 cup rinsed and dried rice to the pan and stir until the grains are coated. Add a little under 2 cups hot chicken or vegetable broth to the rice, bring to a simmer, cover tightly, and cook over very low heat until all the liquid is absorbed. Check after 15 minutes, tasting a few grains for tenderness. If it's undercooked and the broth is absorbed, add a little more, cover the pan, and cook for 2 or 3 minutes more. When the pilaf is finished, add a knob of butter, fluffing the rice up from the bottom with a fork to keep the grains separate.*

## Succotash

This is probably the first truly American dish, one that we learned from the Indians. It also has more regional variations than any other dish; even in the Northeast, the traditional recipe varies from state to state. The one common element is corn and lima beans, a lovely combination that can be embellished in all kinds of ways. But when the limas are from the garden and the corn is fresh from the field, it's best to keep it simple.

Succotash has gotten a bad name because it's so often made with old lima beans from the supermarket and indifferent corn. If that's all you have available, try it with frozen baby limas and shoepeg corn kernels—they're among the few excellent frozen vegetables.

*Serves 4*

1 cup fresh or frozen baby lima beans
salt to taste
1 cup fresh or frozen corn kernels

4 tablespoons (½ stick) butter or
¼ cup heavy cream
freshly ground pepper to taste

In a large saucepan, boil the beans in salted water to cover until nearly done. Add the corn kernels and cook until tender, just a few minutes. Drain, stir in the butter, and check seasoning, adding salt and pepper to taste.

*For fresh ears of corn, scrape the cobs well to get all the delicious milky corn juice.*

*You might want to add a pinch of sugar and a snip of chives.*

*If you want to amplify the dish, you can add a couple of cups of cut-up tomatoes along with the corn. Fry some bacon, then cook some diced onion in the bacon fat and add that to the pot. Crumble the crisp bacon over the top of the dish when it's served, and you have something not dissimilar to the dish Mrs. Abby Fisher, the author of the first known black cookbook in America, listed as Circuit Hash.*

# Creamed Spinach

Spinach and cream have an amazing affinity for each other that sends this dish into the upper register. Made with fresh spinach, it's simply amazing, but even frozen leaf spinach will work. Lots of classic recipes add flour to thicken the mixture or use a white sauce thickened with flour, but we think that's not necessary. Compare this more delicate version with the more familiar floury one, listed in the notes.

This is creamed spinach pure and simple, but you can also add a little lemon juice, some Parmesan, some minced green chiles cooked briefly in the butter, a splash of Madeira, or orange juice. The British food writer Jane Grigson liked to serve creamed spinach with wedges of orange in the middle of the dish so diners could squeeze their own orange juice onto the spinach. She turned this spinach into a course of its own by adding triangles of bread fried crisp in olive oil or butter.

*Serves 6*

3 pounds fresh spinach or 2 (10-
   ounce) packages frozen leaf
   spinach, defrosted
3 tablespoons butter

1 cup heavy cream
freshly grated nutmeg to taste
salt and freshly ground pepper to taste

If you are using fresh spinach, rinse it very well and remove the thick stems. Put it into a very large nonreactive pot over low heat with the lid on. Keep poking the spinach down with a wooden spoon and add more until it all fits into the pot. Raise the heat to medium-high and stir frequently to keep the bottom leaves from sticking and burning. It will take about 10 minutes of cooking altogether—the spinach will be entirely wilted but still bright green.

Drain the spinach thoroughly by pressing it with a wooden spoon against the side of a strainer. Let it cool enough to handle, then squeeze it with your hands to get out the last of the liquid. Blot any remaining liquid with paper towels and chop. (For frozen spinach, cook according to the package directions and drain and chop as just described.)

Melt the butter in a saucepan or skillet over medium heat and add the spinach, mixing well. Add the cream and blend into the spinach until you have just a little sauce. Add a little nutmeg and salt and pepper.

*For a thicker sauce, warm 1 cup cream in a small saucepan and add 1 ta-blespoon flour, whisking over medium heat for a few minutes until the flour is cooked and the sauce is thickened.*

➤ *A little garlic wouldn't be a bad idea, and the subtlest way to do it is to smash a couple of garlic cloves and drop them into the cream, warm it gently, and then let it steep for 10 or 15 minutes. Remove the garlic before adding the cream to the spinach.*

➤ *You could hardly have too much creamed spinach. Leftovers make great fillings for crepes or nests for poached eggs.*

➤ *For a tangy, almost instant creamed spinach, try this recipe from the fifties: Cook frozen spinach and drain well. Sauté ½ chopped onion in 4 tablespoons (½ stick) of butter in a skillet over medium heat and add the spinach, 1 cup sour cream, salt to taste, and 2 teaspoons tarragon vinegar. Mix well and warm briefly before serving.*

Breads

# Boston Brown Bread

This effortless, tasty no-fat quick bread gets a bum rap because of the too-sweet canned variety or because, when it *is* homemade, it's often overcooked and unpleasantly dense. The idea of a "quick" bread clogging up the oven or a burner for 2 hours when it's only a side dish seemed incongruous, so we've turned to the microwave here. Brown bread takes only 5 minutes to prepare and, in the microwave, 18 minutes to cook, which puts it in the category of spur-of-the-moment muffins or biscuits. Nothing is more satisfying than brown bread with a pot of baked beans or a platter of deviled short ribs or smoky ham with sharp mustard. It's also delicious spread with whipped cream cheese for breakfast and, for a nutritious school lunch—pair it with a snappy big red apple.

*Serves 8*

½ cup yellow cornmeal

½ cup whole wheat (graham) flour

½ cup dark rye flour

½ teaspoon salt

¼ cup dark unsulphured molasses

¼ cup pure maple syrup, preferably amber

1 cup buttermilk

½ cup currants or raisins

In a 1-quart glass or ceramic soufflé dish, with a wide wooden spoon, blend all the ingredients well. Cover the dish tightly with plastic wrap, set it in a larger one, and pour 1 inch of hot water into the outer bowl.

Slide the makeshift double boiler into the microwave and cook on medium for 6 minutes. Rotate the dish, microwave for 6 minutes, rotate again, and microwave for a final 6 minutes. Test the bread in the center with a cake tester or a toothpick, right through the wrap. If it's clean, the bread is done. If uncooked batter adheres to it, zap for another 3 minutes. Lift the bread from the water bath and, leaving it covered, let it cool enough to turn out on a bread board. Drape a fresh kitchen towel over it to

Breads

# Boston Brown Bread

This effortless, tasty no-fat quick bread gets a bum rap because of the too-sweet canned variety or because, when it *is* homemade, it's often overcooked and unpleasantly dense. The idea of a "quick" bread clogging up the oven or a burner for 2 hours when it's only a side dish seemed incongruous, so we've turned to the microwave here. Brown bread takes only 5 minutes to prepare and, in the microwave, 18 minutes to cook, which puts it in the category of spur-of-the-moment muffins or biscuits. Nothing is more satisfying than brown bread with a pot of baked beans or a platter of deviled short ribs or smoky ham with sharp mustard. It's also delicious spread with whipped cream cheese for breakfast and, for a nutritious school lunch—pair it with a snappy big red apple.

*Serves 8*

½ cup yellow cornmeal

½ cup whole wheat (graham) flour

½ cup dark rye flour

½ teaspoon salt

¼ cup dark unsulphured molasses

¼ cup pure maple syrup, preferably amber

1 cup buttermilk

½ cup currants or raisins

In a 1-quart glass or ceramic soufflé dish, with a wide wooden spoon, blend all the ingredients well. Cover the dish tightly with plastic wrap, set it in a larger one, and pour 1 inch of hot water into the outer bowl.

Slide the makeshift double boiler into the microwave and cook on medium for 6 minutes. Rotate the dish, microwave for 6 minutes, rotate again, and microwave for a final 6 minutes. Test the bread in the center with a cake tester or a toothpick, right through the wrap. If it's clean, the bread is done. If uncooked batter adheres to it, zap for another 3 minutes. Lift the bread from the water bath and, leaving it covered, let it cool enough to turn out on a bread board. Drape a fresh kitchen towel over it to keep it moist and either slice and serve while it's still warm or wrap and store. Brown bread keeps in the refrigerator for about 10 days.

*➤ Brown bread is wonderful lightly toasted.*

*➤ If your rye or whole wheat flour has been on the shelf for a while, give it a good sniff to be sure it's not rancid. Dark flours spoil quickly and should be stored in the refrigerator.*

*➤ If you prefer to steam the bread in the classic manner, pour the batter into a clean well-buttered coffee can and cover it with a bonnet of foil tied tightly around the can with string. Stand it in a deep pot and pour in enough boiling water to come two thirds of the way up the can. When the water is simmering gently, cover the pot, turn the heat to low, and steam the bread for 2 hours and 15 minutes. For the most consistently even low heat, steaming in the oven at 300° for 2½ hours is preferable to the stovetop.*

## Cinnamon Walnut Coffee Cake

This deliciously simple coffee cake made its debut in the fifties and spread like wildfire—it turns up in regional cookbooks all over the country. It's rich and delectable, which is no doubt why it's survived. If you plan to serve it to company, bake it in a pretty tin or ceramic pan since you'll have to cut and serve it from the pan.

*Serves 10*

½ pound (2 sticks) unsalted butter at
   room temperature
1¼ cups plus 2 tablespoons sugar
2 large eggs at room temperature
1 cup sour cream
2 cups flour

½ teaspoon baking soda
1½ teaspoons baking powder
1 teaspoon pure vanilla extract
¾ cup finely chopped walnuts
1 teaspoon ground cinnamon

Do not preheat the oven. Have ready a 10-inch buttered and floured tube pan.

Combine the butter, 1¼ cups sugar, and the eggs in an electric mixer or a large mixing bowl and beat until light and fluffy. Add the sour cream and blend well. Add the flour, baking soda, and baking powder and stir well. Add the vanilla and stir again.

Spoon half of the batter into the pan. Mix the walnuts, cinnamon, and remaining sugar together in a small bowl. Sprinkle half the nut mixture over the batter. Spoon in the remaining batter and top with the rest of the nut mixture.

Place the cake on the middle shelf of a cold oven, set the temperature to 350°, and bake for about 55 minutes, until golden brown on top and a toothpick inserted in the center comes out dry. Cool on a rack briefly, then cut in the pan to serve warm or cool—warm is best.

➷ Pecans may be even better than walnuts here.

➷ Like all quick breads, this cake doesn't keep too well; eat it the first day.

# Popovers

*L*ike piecrust, the mere mention of popovers seems to drop a veil of wistful self-doubt over the faces of otherwise confident cooks. That's odd because actually they're not tricky to make. A perfect popover is more like a triumph over nature than a matter of skill. Your 5-minute contribution of time involves carefully measuring and quickly mixing ingredients and using an oven thermometer if there's any doubt about your oven's calibration. Not a big deal for a delicious bread that never fails to bring applause at the table. The worst that can happen is that you underbake them and have a little more soft, eggy batter inside than you'd like, but having none at all is like eating a burned fried egg.

*Serves 8*

2 large eggs

1 cup milk

¼ teaspoon salt

1 tablespoon butter, melted

1 cup flour, lightly scooped

cooking spray

Preheat the oven to 425°. Set 8 glass custard cups on a cookie sheet and slide them into the oven to preheat. Or use a popover pan with metal cups hung on a steel-rod frame. Muffin tins don't conduct enough heat to do the best job. Whisk together the eggs, milk, salt, and melted butter. Add the flour, one half at a time, and mix until fairly smooth. Leaving a few tiny lumps is better than overbeating. Remove the cups or pan from the oven when it has preheated and spray each cup well with cooking spray (butter will burn). Fill the cups a little more than halfway.

Carefully slide the pan into the oven and bake for 20 minutes. Reduce the heat to 375° and bake for another 15 to 20 minutes. Peek after 30 minutes, not before. They're done when the crust is an even rich brown with no visible walls of uncooked dough. Pull the oven shelf out and pierce the popovers at their waists with the tip of a paring knife or stick them with a fork. Turn the heat off and leave the door ajar.

Leaving them in a warm oven for 5 to 10 minutes will dry out any excess interior moisture. Serve the popovers hot, slathered with sweet butter.

&#10148; *Since there's no leavening, the batter can sit for as long as you want. You can even mix it the night before and refrigerate it if you need a jump start on breakfast.*

&#10148; *Popovers are at their steamy best when served straight from the oven, but they can be made an hour or so ahead of time and reheated briefly in a moderate oven. They'll hold their shape perfectly. They can also be baked, frozen, and re-heated.*

&#10148; *We used to start popovers in a cold oven, as many cookbooks advise, but we've switched to the hot oven method with much more consistent success.*

&#10148; VARIATIONS: *This is the same batter for making a Dutch Baby. Simply pour the full recipe into a 10-inch round slope-sided gratin dish or skillet that has been preheated in a 425° oven with 3 tablespoons of butter and bake for 20 minutes, then reduce the heat to 350° and bake for 20 minutes longer. Serve*

---

### *Garlic Bread*

*Who could forget the tempting perfume of thick slices of bakery French bread slathered with savory garlic butter? If this delight no longer seems an accept-able indulgence, try brushing the bread with olive oil, garlic, and lots of minced fresh herbs like thyme and oregano or rosemary. Sprinkle with freshly grated Parmesan cheese before grilling, broiling, or baking. Or mix minced cilantro, chives, garlic, and ginger with safflower oil spiked with a dash of chili oil or Thai chili sauce and a few drops of toasted sesame oil.*

*with jam or maple syrup or top the pancake with apple slices sautéed in butter and sprinkle with a little finely grated sharp aged Cheddar.*

*The American Heritage Cookbook has a recipe for chicken pudding taken from an old family cookbook of President James Monroe. The popover batter is baked over chicken pieces that are first browned, then simmered in chicken broth. The "pudding" is served with a pan gravy. You might like to experiment with this idea, using fresh herbs in the batter and seasoning the braised chicken with a squeeze of fresh lemon juice and a few whole garlic cloves. Or use left-over roast chicken and make a light gravy of sautéed minced shallots, garlic and herbs, a little instant flour to thicken, and homemade or canned chicken broth.*

## Scones

These wonderfully rich British cousins of biscuits are foolproof and make a special occasion out of breakfast or tea. Serve them right out of the oven; scones don't keep well. The British, by the way, say "skonz," not "skohnes."

*Makes 12 scones*

**The Dry Ingredients:**

2 cups flour

2 teaspoons baking powder

1 tablespoon sugar

½ teaspoon salt

4 tablespoons (½ stick) cold unsalted
   butter, diced

**The Wet Ingredients:**

2 large eggs

½ cup light or heavy cream

½ teaspoon pure vanilla extract

Preheat the oven to 425°. Lightly butter a baking sheet and set aside.

Using a whisk, mix the dry ingredients well in a mixing bowl. Work in the butter with a wooden spoon until you have a mealy texture. In a separate bowl, mix the wet ingredients, then pour them into the flour mixture. Stir together just enough to moisten the dough. On a lightly floured work surface, knead the dough gently until it just comes together—about 10 turns. Shape it into a circle about ¾ inch thick, then brush the top with a little more cream or milk and sprinkle with sugar. Cut the circle into 12 wedges and place them on the baking sheet. Bake for about 15 minutes, until just golden.

*You can add all sorts of interesting tidbits: a handful of currants, ½ cup of diced candied ginger, orange zest, dried cherries plumped for 15 minutes in a little orange juice.*

# Hush Puppies

The old story is that Southern cooks used to quiet the dogs by frying up little dollops of corn bread batter and tossing them to the beasts. Whatever their origin, these little deep-fried nuggets are addictive. The recipe comes from James Villas, superlative Southern cook. Hush puppies are perfect with fried fish or barbecue.

*Serves 8*

2 cups flour

1½ cups stone-ground white
   cornmeal

3 tablespoons sugar

1 teaspoon baking powder

1 teaspoon salt

½ cup finely minced onion

1⅓ cups milk

⅓ cup vegetable oil

1 large egg, beaten

corn or vegetable oil for deep frying

Have lots of paper towels ready for draining the hush puppies once they're fried.

Into a large mixing bowl, sift together the flour, cornmeal, sugar, baking powder, and salt and blend thoroughly. Add the onion, milk, oil, and egg and stir long enough to blend well, adding a little cold water if necessary to make the batter a good dropping consistency.

In a deep-fat fryer or deep cast-iron skillet, heat about 2½ inches of oil to 375°. If you don't have a thermometer, the oil will be ready when a faint blue haze rises from the surface—don't let the oil smoke, or you'll have to start over with a new batch of oil. Drop the batter by tablespoons into the fat and fry till the hush puppies are golden brown and crisp. Drain on the paper towels and serve immediately.

## Irish Soda Bread

There are many kinds of Irish soda bread—with all whole wheat flour, with bran, with oats—but this American one (which has more baking powder than baking soda) is the easiest, since there's no kneading or sifting, and it's also delicious. It will be hard not to eat this bread straight out of the oven, but refrain until it's cool; it will slice much better, and you want thin slices. It also toasts beautifully, but keeps only a day or two.

You can bake the bread in a standard loaf pan or shape it into the classic round loaf and bake it on a cookie sheet or baking stone. It's traditional to cut a cross into the top to let the fairies out, say the Irish.

*Serves 10*

1 large egg, beaten

2 cups buttermilk

¼ teaspoon baking soda

3½ cups flour

1 cup raisins

2 tablespoons caraway seeds
   (optional)

¼ cup sugar

1 teaspoon salt

1 tablespoon plus 1 teaspoon baking
   powder

Preheat the oven to 375°. Grease and flour a loaf pan or have a baking sheet or baking stone ready.

Combine the first 3 ingredients in a large bowl and set aside. With your hands, mix together the remaining ingredients in a separate bowl. Add the dry ingredients to the buttermilk mixture and mix just until they're blended.

Plop the dough into the loaf pan or shape it into a round loaf on the baking sheet. Use a knife to cut a cross in the top. Bake for 1 hour and 15 minutes or until the center is moist but not too doughy when tested with a fork. If the top seems to be getting brown too fast, cover it with foil for the rest of the baking time. Let it cool on a rack for at least 30 minutes.

# Corn Bread

*P*eople get passionate about corn bread. Southerners say it has to be made with bacon grease, preferably using white cornmeal with no wheat flour, and it must on no account have any sugar added. Yankees like their corn bread more like cake, with a fine crumb and a pronounced sweetness. (A little sweetness can also cover for any bitterness in the cornmeal.) That means using some wheat flour and losing the tang of buttermilk, which makes the Southern version so distinctive.

Both camps agree that skillet corn bread is the way to go. Here's Charleston cook John Taylor's superb skillet corn bread, the easiest one we know, along with a Yankee version that also works for vegetarians.

The most important element for either version is the cornmeal itself: You want stone-ground cornmeal, whatever color you prefer. Keep it in the refrigerator since it quickly develops an off flavor on the shelf.

*Serves 6*

4 strips of bacon

1 large egg

2 cups buttermilk

1¾ cups stone-ground cornmeal,
   yellow or white

1 scant teaspoon baking powder

1 scant teaspoon salt

1 scant teaspoon baking soda

Fry the bacon in a 9- or 10-inch cast-iron skillet. (Southerners specify a never-washed well-seasoned skillet, but your regular old cast-iron skillet will be fine too.) Drain the cooked bacon and set aside—it can be a cook's treat or you can crumble it and add it to the batter just before baking the corn bread. Save the bacon grease and measure 2 teaspoons back into the skillet. Film the bottom and sides of the skillet with the bacon grease and put it in the oven. Preheat the oven to 450°.

Meanwhile, mix the egg into the buttermilk, then add the cornmeal and beat it into the batter. When the skillet is almost smoking and the oven has reached 450°, add the remaining ingredients and beat them in well—including the bacon bits if you're using them.

Pour the batter into the hot skillet and bake for 15 to 20 minutes or until the top just begins to brown. Loosen the edges with a spatula and turn out the corn bread onto a plate to serve hot. Or cut it right in the skillet and serve the wedges individually.

Leftover corn bread will keep, well wrapped in foil, for a day—but it's never as good as when it comes straight from the oven.

➥ *You can of course add grated cheese, minced jalapeño peppers, chopped red or green bell peppers, corn kernels, and any number of other tidbits to your corn bread.*

➥

## Yankee Corn Bread

| | |
|---|---|
| 2 large eggs | 1½ tablespoons white vinegar |
| 3 tablespoons butter, melted | 1 cup flour |
| 3 tablespoons sugar | ¾ cup stone-ground yellow cornmeal |
| ½ teaspoon salt | 1 teaspoon baking powder |
| 2 cups milk | ½ teaspoon baking soda |

Preheat the oven to 350°. Butter an 8-inch square baking dish and set it in the oven to heat while you mix the batter.

Put the eggs in a mixing bowl and add the butter. Beat until well blended and add the sugar, salt, milk, and vinegar, beating well.

In a bowl, stir together the remaining ingredients, then add them to the egg mixture. Mix just until the batter is smooth and there are no lumps.

Pour the batter into the heated baking dish and bake for 1 hour or until lightly browned. Serve warm.

VARIATION: *Try Marjorie Kinnan Rawlings's (yes, the author) great idea of adding 1 cup heavy cream to this corn bread—just pour the cream into the center of the batter in the baking dish right before it goes into the oven and don't stir it. This corn bread has a delectable creamy center.*

## Buttermilk Biscuits

These buttermilk drop biscuits find their own shape in the oven, so you don't have to roll them out and cut them. They're tender and delicious and the work of a moment. Your object here is to produce extremely light, moist biscuits; dropped biscuits are lightest, and vegetable shortening makes them even lighter—but you can use butter if you'd rather.

### Makes 1 dozen 3-inch biscuits

2 cups flour
1 tablespoon baking powder
1/2 teaspoon baking soda

1/2 teaspoon salt
1/3 cup vegetable shortening, chilled
1 1/3 cups buttermilk

Preheat the oven to 500°. Lightly butter a baking sheet.

Using a whisk, mix together the dry ingredients in a mixing bowl. Add the shortening and cut it into the flour with a pastry blender until it looks mealy. Add the buttermilk and stir it with a fork just until the mixture is moistened and the dough cleans the sides of the bowl.

Drop the dough by spoonfuls onto the baking sheet. The closer together the biscuits are, the higher they'll rise. Bake for 8 to 10 minutes or until golden brown and serve immediately.

&#10148; For the traditional rolled and cut biscuit, use only 1 cup buttermilk and turn out the dough onto a lightly floured work surface. Knead it as little and as lightly as possible—about 5 turns. Pat it into a circle ½ inch thick. Using a biscuit cutter or an inverted glass, cut into 3-inch rounds, being careful not to twist the cutter. Gather the scraps and cut them too.

&#10148; If you have access to Southern flour—White Lily is a good brand—by all means use it; it's much softer, and your biscuits will be even lighter.

&#10148; If you're using the biscuits for shortcake, add a tablespoon of sugar to the dry ingredients.

&#10148; For breakfast biscuits, you can get a head start by mixing up the dry ingredients the night before.

&#10148; Southerners traditionally pull their biscuits apart rather than cutting them with a knife, the better to appreciate their texture.

## Blueberry Muffins

Thanks to the temperate climate of South America, we can have blueberry muffins year-round. In winter, Chilean berries are huge and scrumptious. You can even mail-order tiny, wild Maine blueberries from L. L. Bean. This recipe counts on juicy, ripe berries for natural sweetness and country flavor. The muffins keep well, but because they're very moist, they should be warmed in the oven (never the microwave) before serving. They need only a tad of butter to be perfect.

*Makes 1 dozen*

**The Wet Ingredients:**

1 large egg

1 cup buttermilk

1 teaspoon pure vanilla extract

6 tablespoons (¾ stick) unsalted
   butter, melted

**The Dry Ingredients:**

2 cups flour

1 teaspoon baking soda

pinch of salt

½ cup sugar

freshly grated nutmeg to taste
   (optional)

1½ cups blueberries, rinsed and
   drained

Preheat the oven to 375° and butter or spray a 12-cup muffin tin with oil. Beat the wet ingredients in a small bowl with a whisk or hand mixer until very well blended. Loosely scoop the flour before measuring into a large mixing bowl—save out a spoonful for the berries. Add the rest of the dry ingredients and mix well with a fork or whisk, making a well in the center. Add the liquid ingredients and blend the batter lightly and briefly, just to combine. Roll the berries on paper towels to dry and dust very lightly with the spoonful of flour. Fold them into the batter and immediately fill the muffin tin. Bake for 20 minutes and cool on a wire rack.

# Bran Muffins

We don't even care that they're good for you—these are really delicious bran muffins with a moist, cakey crumb and a hint of spice to give them character.

*Makes 1 dozen*

1 large egg

1 cup plain yogurt

1 teaspoon pure vanilla extract

6 tablespoons (¾ stick) unsalted
   butter, melted

½ cup packed light brown sugar

1 cup flour

1 cup unprocessed bran flakes

1 teaspoon baking soda

½ teaspoon baking powder

1 teaspoon ground cinnamon
   (optional)

pinch of ground cloves (optional)

½ cup currants or golden raisins

Preheat the oven to 375° and line a 12-cup muffin tin with paper muffin cups. Mix the egg, yogurt, vanilla, butter, and sugar with a whisk or hand mixer until well blended. Loosely scoop the flour before measuring into a large mixing bowl. Add the rest of the ingredients except the currants and mix thoroughly with a fork or whisk. Make a well in the center and add the wet ingredients. Blend the batter lightly and briefly, just to combine. Quickly fold in the currants or raisins. Fill the muffin cups and bake for 20 minutes. Cool in the pan for 15 minutes, then transfer to a wire rack to cool completely.

# Buttermilk Pancakes

*I*f you memorize this recipe, you can have buttermilk pancakes any old time, in less time, in fact, than it takes to decide this is the night to have them for supper with a couple of spicy sausages.

*Serves 4*

**The Wet Ingredients:**

1 cup buttermilk

1 large egg

4 tablespoons (½ stick) butter, melted

**The Dry Ingredients:**

1 cup flour

pinch of salt

1 teaspoon baking soda

In a large bowl, whisk together the wet ingredients until well blended. In a small bowl, blend the dry ingredients with a fork to distribute them. Add the dry ingredients to the wet ingredients, stirring very briefly to moisten the flour. Don't worry about lumps. Spread the batter onto a well-greased hot griddle and cook over medium-high heat until bubbles appear and the surface of the pancake is no longer wet. Turn and cook briefly on the other side.

*Drop a few blueberries onto each pancake as soon as they hit the griddle or stir grated apple and a dash of cinnamon into the batter.*

## *Rhode Island Johnnycakes*

*These are a good breakfast alternative to pancakes and much simpler to make. Combine 1½ cups stone-ground cornmeal, yellow or white, with 1 teaspoon salt and 2 tablespoons soft butter. Slowly stir in 1½ cups boiling water, stirring continuously until the water is incorporated. Add ½ cup milk and beat. Ladle ¼ cup of the batter onto a hot well-buttered griddle, leaving room for the cakes to spread. Fry for about 3 minutes on each side or until the johnnycake is crispy at the edges and well browned. If the batter is too thick to make a crispy cake, thin it with a little more milk. Serve with melted butter and maple syrup.*

## Quick Waffles

ow many times have you been in the mood for waffles on Sunday morning but too lazy to start digging into your library for a good recipe? There are so many variations, but this is an easy basic waffle guaranteed to satisfy that whim. If you use one more than twice a year, the new nonstick waffle irons with accurate thermostats are well worth the investment.

*Serves 4*

2 large eggs, well beaten

1¼ cups milk

3 tablespoons butter, melted, or
   vegetable oil

1 tablespoon sugar

1 teaspoon pure vanilla extract
   (optional)

¼ teaspoon salt

1½ cups flour

2 teaspoons baking powder

Preheat the waffle iron. Whisk the beaten eggs with the milk, butter, sugar, and vanilla. Whisk the dry ingredients in a large bowl and add the wet ingredients. Blend briefly to combine. Let the batter rest for a few minutes before pouring it onto the griddle, stopping about ½ inch before it reaches the edge so it doesn't spill over.

*For crispier waffles, separate the eggs, beat the egg whites until stiff, and fold them into the batter.*

*For a nice corn crunch, substitute ½ cup cornmeal for ½ cup of the flour.*

*For a deep corn flavor, use half masa harina and half flour.*

*For buttermilk waffles, use an amount equal to sweet milk and add a pinch of baking soda.*

*For spicy waffles, add ½ teaspoon ground cinnamon and several gratings of fresh nutmeg.*

*If you want to add chopped nuts, sprinkle them over the batter just before they're done to preserve their crispiness.*

*To beat the clock, mix the dry ingredients the night before. In the morning, while the waffle iron is heating, melt the butter and sugar together in the microwave and whisk together the wet ingredients. Add the warm butter to the egg mixture, whisking briskly to bring everything to room temperature. Combine with the dry ingredients.*

Desserts

# Apple Crisp

This delectable old-time dessert comes to mind the very day local apples begin tumbling from the produce stand. The sweet aroma of a baking apple crisp is as good as it gets, but we're also very fond of using half pears. If you want to try it, the ginger preserves are worth tracking down. We've used our favorite nut in the topping, but the more common walnut is equally good.

*Serves 6*

### The Fruit:

6 crisp firm apples, mixed varieties if possible, or half apples and half pears

¼ cup pure maple syrup

2 teaspoons fresh lemon juice

1 tablespoon ginger preserves (optional)

### The Topping:

¾ cup flour

½ cup packed light brown sugar

¼ teaspoon ground cinnamon

¼ teaspoon ground ginger

pinch of salt

6 tablespoons (¾ stick) butter, cut into cubes

¾ cup chopped pecans

Preheat the oven to 400°. Lightly butter the inside of a 10-inch ceramic gratin dish or pie plate. Peel, core, and thickly slice the fruit. Layer it in the dish, fitting the slices in as tightly as possible. Drizzle the fruit with the maple syrup and lemon juice. Cover the dish tightly with plastic wrap and cook the fruit in the microwave on HIGH for 5 minutes. Uncover the dish, let it cool slightly, and pour off the accumulated liquid into a small skillet, adding the ginger preserves if desired. Cook the juices and preserves over medium-high heat until they reduce down to a light syrupy glaze. Drizzle the glaze back over the fruit.

Put the flour, sugar, cinnamon, ginger, and salt in a food processor and pulse to blend. Add the butter and pulse to reduce the butter to pea-sized bits. Turn out into a bowl and add the chopped nuts. Mix everything together with your fingertips until the topping is lumpy. Cover the fruit with the topping and bake for 20 minutes.

*Precooking the fruit slightly not only solves the problem of excess juice sending up steam to make the crispy topping soggy but also cuts the cooking time in half. If you don't have a microwave, bake the crisp for 40 minutes and pour off the excess juice before serving.*

*Filling the spaces between the fruit slices with raw cranberries makes a colorful and festive holiday crisp, particularly with mixed fruit. A light and lovely alternative to pie on the groaning board.*

*You can use other sweeteners for the fruit. Flavored honeys work well; we like ginger-lemon honey. Try apple or currant jelly melted with a little dark rum or calvados. Not classic, of course, but mighty good.*

## Blintzes

*Now that you can buy Frieda's Finest and Master Chef crêpes in a package in many supermarkets, you can quickly make blintzes by filling them with 1 pound sieved low-fat (1%) cottage cheese mixed with 2 tablespoons sour cream, 1 egg yolk, 2 tablespoons sugar, 1 teaspoon pure vanilla extract, and a pinch of salt. Blend well in a food processor, fill each crêpe with about 3 tablespoons of the cheese mixture, and roll them up Chinese egg roll fashion. Fry them in butter in a nonstick skillet over medium-high heat, removing them as soon as they're golden brown. Serve with sour cream topping for a great brunch, lunch, or late-night supper.*

# Pound Cake

his simplest of all cakes is perhaps the most delicious. It's a great keeper—in fact, you shouldn't even dip into it until the day after it's baked—and it goes with almost everything. If you have a pound cake tucked away, and some good ice cream in the freezer, all you have to do is smear a slice of cake with some sweet butter, toast it, and top with ice cream for a sensational dessert.

There are all kinds of ways to flavor pound cakes, but we think citrus zest is perhaps best of all, along with a little brandy. Sherry and mace are great, too.

This is a really easy cake to make—just be sure your eggs are warm, you beat the butter and sugar long enough so that the batter is really fluffy, and once the flour goes in, don't overmix or the cake will be tough.

*Serves 16*

2 cups sifted flour

¼ teaspoon salt

¼ teaspoon ground mace (optional)

1 tablespoon grated lemon zest (optional)

1 teaspoon grated orange zest (optional)

1⅓ cups sugar

½ pound (2 sticks) butter at room temperature

5 large eggs, warmed in water in their shells

1 tablespoon pure vanilla extract

juice of 1 lemon

2 tablespoons sherry or brandy (optional)

½ cup half-and-half

Preheat the oven to 325°. Have ready a greased and floured tube or bundt pan.

Mix the flour, salt, and mace in a small bowl and whisk together to blend. Set aside.

In a food processor fitted with the metal blade, mix the citrus zest with the sugar.

*178*

Using an electric mixer, cream the butter on low speed until it's very light and fluffy. Slowly add the citrus sugar by the spoonful and beat until fluffy, at least 5 minutes. Scrape the bowl and beaters down several times during the creaming.

Add the eggs one by one. After the third egg goes in, scrape the bowl and add 2 tablespoons of the flour mixture. Stop and scrape again. Add the vanilla, lemon juice, and sherry.

Mix in the flour by hand, in thirds, alternating with the half-and-half. Don't overmix. Spread the batter evenly in the pan and spank it sharply on the counter to eliminate any air bubbles.

Bake for I hour on the middle shelf of the oven. Check after 50 minutes to see if the cake is done—the top will spring back when you touch it. Cool the cake in its pan for 15 minutes, then turn it out onto a rack. When thoroughly cooled, wrap in foil and store in a tightly sealed container. Don't slice for 24 hours. Pound cakes will keep beautifully in the freezer for months.

*Some Southerners complain about pound cakes with a "sad streak," a runny valley down the middle. Others claim to prefer them that way. To avoid a sad streak, turn the oven off when the cake is done and crack the oven door a little. Let the cake rest in the oven for another 30 minutes before removing.*

*You can put in half the batter, then scatter chocolate chips and chopped pecans or walnuts over; spread the rest of the batter on top and scatter more chocolate and nuts over before the cake goes in the oven.*

*For richer flavor try making the cake with half butter, half cream cheese.*

*Make a lemon glaze for the cake: While it's still hot, mix 1/3 cup fresh lemon juice with 3/4 cup sugar. Stir together and brush all over the cake.*

*Instead of citrus, mace, and brandy, flavor the cake with 1 teaspoon almond extract.*

# Applesauce Cake

For those of us lucky enough to have a mother who bakes, applesauce cake is one of the most cherished after-school snack memories. These simple, flavorful cakes have come around to popularity again, and in our opinion they should stay there. They need no icing, they travel well, they wrap beautifully for gifting, they're not too decadent for between-meal snacking—and a fat slice is perfect for breakfast-on-the-run.

*Serves 8*

¼ pound (1 stick) butter

1 cup packed dark brown sugar

1 extra-large egg

2 cups unsifted flour

2 teaspoons baking powder

1 teaspoon baking soda

½ teaspoon salt

1 teaspoon ground cinnamon

½ teaspoon ground mace

½ teaspoon freshly grated nutmeg

1 cup unsweetened applesauce

2 teaspoons instant coffee powder (optional)

½ cup raisins, plumped in dark rum

¾ cup chopped toasted pecans

Preheat the oven to 350°. Spray a 9- by 5-inch loaf pan with cooking spray. Cream the butter in a stand or hand mixer. Add the sugar and beat until fluffy and the sugar is mostly dissolved. Add the egg and combine well. Sift the dry ingredients and add to the creamed mixture alternately with the applesauce mixed with the powdered coffee (which will darken the cake beautifully and intensify its flavors). When the batter is velvety, fold in the rummy raisins and the toasted pecans. Bake for 55 minutes or until a cake tester or toothpick comes out clean. Cool on a wire rack.

# Carrot Cake

The original carrot cakes came from Austria and had a refined delicate character quite unlike the dense, heavy version that's become an American classic. The advent of the food processor has made carrot cakes a snap, since you can grate the carrots and chop the nuts in moments. Carrot cakes keep very well, and their flavor develops with time.

*Serves 10*

2 cups sugar

1½ cups vegetable oil

4 large eggs at room temperature

2 cups flour

2 teaspoons ground cinnamon

1 teaspoon baking soda

½ teaspoon salt

3 cups grated carrots, about 4 large carrots

1 cup chopped pecans

**The Icing:**

6 ounces cream cheese at room temperature

6 tablespoons (¾ stick) butter at room temperature

2½ heaped cups confectioners' sugar, sifted

1 teaspoon pure vanilla extract

Preheat the oven to 350°. Grease a tube or bundt pan.

Beat the sugar with the oil in a large mixing bowl until combined. Add the eggs and beat again to combine. Mix together the dry ingredients and add to the mixture. Beat to combine, then add the carrots and pecans.

Pour the batter into the pan and bake for 1 hour or longer, until a toothpick inserted in the center comes out dry.

Let the cake cool on a rack, then remove from the pan to a serving plate. Cream the icing ingredients together in a bowl until they're spreadable. Frost the cake.

☞ *Needless to say, you don't have to ice the cake at all. Just sift a little powdered sugar on top and you're all set.*

☞ *You can make carrot cake muffins with this recipe. Spoon the batter into muffin tins, filling them half full. Bake for about 25 minutes or until a toothpick inserted in the center comes out dry.*

## Angel Food Cake

It is the world's lightest cake—the polar opposite of wickedly rich devil's food cake—and it's also amazingly easy to make, despite its reputation for being tricky. There are just a couple of caveats; see the notes at the end of the recipe. This is the only cake we can think of that doesn't require greasing the pan—in fact, it's forbidden. And we should also point out that this cake has no fat whatsoever, in case you care. But that's not the reason to make it—people love this cake, and a homemade angel food cake is a great treat.

*Serves 8*

1 cup flour
1½ cups superfine sugar
12 large egg whites at room
    temperature

½ teaspoon salt
1 teaspoon pure vanilla extract
½ teaspoon almond extract (optional)
1½ teaspoons cream of tartar

Preheat the oven to 325°. You'll need a 10-inch tube pan with a removable bottom or a 10-inch springform pan that's at least 3 inches deep. Be sure the pan, beaters, and bowl are scrupulously clean, or the egg whites won't rise to their full volume and your cake won't be as ethereal.

Mix the flour and half the sugar in a mixing bowl using a wire whisk. Set aside.

Put the egg whites in a mixing bowl if you're beating them by hand or in the bowl of the electric mixer if you're using it. Add the salt, vanilla, and almond extract if you're using it. Beat the egg whites until they're just beginning to froth, then sprinkle the cream of tartar over them and continue beating until you have stiff glossy peaks. Add the remaining sugar, ¼ cup at a time.

Add the flour mixture to the egg whites gradually, sprinkling it over the top and folding it in with a rubber spatula.

Gently push the batter into the ungreased pan and run a knife through it all the way around the cake in the center. Smooth out the top with the knife. Bake for 40 to 45 minutes or until the top springs back when you touch it.

Remove the cake from the oven and cool it—if your pan has legs, invert it onto the legs. If not, hang it upside down over the neck of a large bottle. It will take 1½ hours to cool completely. Run a knife around the edge of the pan and the center tube to loosen the cake, then invert it onto a serving plate. To cut the cake, use 2 forks to gently pull it apart.

> *The almond extract is optional, but we'd really miss the flavor.*

> *For the lightest, airiest cake, try Marion Cunningham's trick of beating the egg whites with 2 tablespoons cold water.*

> *Almost all recipes for this cake require cake flour, and you can use it, of course, but cake flour makes a difference in a recipe only if you're using baking powder; this cake is leavened by air whipped into the whites, so cake flour isn't essential.*

> *A crucial point: Have everything extremely clean so the egg whites can incorporate a maximum amount of air (any fat will inhibit them, including bits of yolk creeping in). Don't beat the egg whites in a plastic bowl.*

> *You can leave out the cream of tartar, but be careful not to overbeat the egg whites or they'll dry out.*

&rarr; *Chocolate fiends can substitute ¼ cup cocoa (Hershey's is fine here) for the same amount of flour. Or they can add 1 cup of chocolate chips just before the cake goes into the pan.*

&rarr; *Sylvia Balser Hirsch, the owner of the famous Miss Grimble's bakery in New York City, had a secret weapon at home for emergency dessert: She just added 2 to 3 tablespoons instant coffee powder (not freeze-dried) to Duncan Hines angel food cake mix. For frosting, she beat ¼ pound (1 stick) soft unsalted butter with 3 cups sifted confectioners' sugar and added a pinch of salt, ¼ cup milk, and 3 tablespoons instant coffee powder. She topped the frosted cake with ½ cup of sliced toasted almonds and called the whole thing her Instant Genius Cake.*

&rarr; *This cake needs no embellishing, but you can sift a little powdered sugar on top along with some grated orange zest. Or make a thin icing with sifted confectioners' sugar blended with orange or lemon juice and spread it over the top of the cake.*

&rarr;

### Macaroons

*Preheat the oven to 350°. Crumble an 8-ounce can of almond paste into a food processor and add ½ cup confectioners' sugar, 2 large egg whites, a pinch of salt, and ½ teaspoon pure vanilla extract. Process until smooth. Pipe into well-separated rounds through a pastry tube (or cut off the corner tip of a freezer storage bag) on a baking sheet sprayed with cooking oil or covered with parchment paper. Bake for 15 to 20 minutes or until lightly colored. Cool on wire racks. These cookies will keep for weeks in an airtight container in the refrigerator.*

# Cheesecake

$\mathscr{S}$ ome 20 recipes and nearly as many pounds later, here's what we've learned: You need a sturdy 9- or 10-inch springform pan. You don't need a bottom crust, and unless you're a baroque worrier and the idea of a possible hairline crack would freak you out, you don't need to bake the cake in a water bath. Finally, unless you're a New Yorker who pledges allegiance to the Jewish cheesecake, this recipe is unparalleled. It's somewhere between the European fresh-curd cheesecake and the American cream cheese version.

*Serves 10 to 12*

soft butter for greasing pan

½ cup cinnamon graham cracker
   crumbs

1¼ cups plus 2 tablespoons superfine
   sugar

1 package Petit Beurre cookies or
   Destrooper Almond Thins from
   Holland

1 15-ounce carton ricotta cheese

3 tablespoons flour

pinch of salt

1½ pounds Philadelphia cream
   cheese, softened

1 tablespoon pure vanilla extract

finely grated zest of 2 lemons

4 extra-large eggs at room
   temperature

2 cups sour cream at room
   temperature

Preheat the oven to 350°. Very generously butter the inside of a 9- or 10-inch springform pan. Mix the graham cracker crumbs with the 2 tablespoons sugar and sprinkle it in the pan, rotating it to stick to the butter and pressing it in to cover. Gently shake out any loose crumbs. Lay the cookies on the bottom of the pan. Never mind the resulting spaces in between. If you're using the paper-thin almond cookies, there will be plenty of broken ones in the box that can fill in the holes. Don't fuss—this layer merely assures that the bottom of the cake will release more easily when cut. Refrigerate the prepared pan while you make the filling.

Smooth the ricotta cheese in the food processor or push it through a fine-mesh sieve if you have time to spare. Mix the 1¼ cups sugar, flour, and salt. Cream the cream cheese and sugar mixture in a stand mixer on low speed for about 2 minutes. Scrape down the sides of the bowl. You don't want to beat air into this batter, so keep the speed of the mixer on low throughout. Add the ricotta cheese and continue blending until the batter is smooth. Scrape the bowl again. Blend in the vanilla and the lemon zest. Add the eggs one at a time scraping down the bowl, and blending after each addition. Blend in the sour cream. Taste the mixture. If you reach for a big spoon, you'll know it's perfect. If you'd like it more lemony, add a little lemon extract or pure lemon oil (Boyajian).

Put the prepared springform pan on a cookie sheet and carefully pour in the mixture. If you have a 9-inch pan, the mixture should be ½ inch from the top. In a 10-inch pan there will be plenty of room for the slight rise. Gently slide the pan onto the middle oven rack. Put a shallow pan of hot tap water on the shelf below. Keeping the oven moist will prevent unsightly surface cracks. (You can forget the pan of water and simply spray the sides of the hot oven with water before inserting the cake and again after 30 minutes.)

Resist opening the oven for 30 minutes. If the top is browning when you do, rest a sheet of foil on it. Only the edges of the cake should color. Check again in 20 minutes. The cake is done when the center still jiggles. Don't try determining this with a cake tester. It will always pull out with batter stuck to it because cheesecake finally sets up only when chilled. A cake in a 9-inch pan takes longer to cook than in a 10-inch pan with the same amount of batter.

When the cake is done, in about an hour, turn off the heat and leave it in the oven with the door ajar for another hour. Cracks might appear if the cake either overcooks or cools down too quickly. Pull the cake from the oven, run a sharp knife around the inside edge of the pan so the cake can contract naturally, and let it cool further at room temperature and away from drafts. Then cover the top with foil or plastic wrap and refrigerate overnight. When the cake is cold, release the latch on the pan and remove the ring. Don't attempt to remove the cake from the bottom insert until it's half gone.

≈ The easiest way to cut cheesecake is with a long piece of dental floss, slicing down and pulling the string out from the bottom. Otherwise, use a large, sharp knife dipped in very hot water between cuts.

≈ If you're buying a springform pan, check out the new glass-bottom German one made by Zenker. It's cleverly designed to prevent the cake from sticking to the bottom.

≈ If you can find cake boards at your paper supply store or local bakery, cover one with foil and set it over the removable bottom of the springform. When the cake is cold, you can release it from the pan altogether and you'll have a base for both storage and serving.

≈ We like this cake plain or with fresh berries. Syrupy fruit toppings make it look and taste banal.

# Gingerbread

*M*ost gingerbread recipes are just good spice cakes. We think gingerbread ought to be distinctly gingery and bitey, not just enticingly dark and aromatic. So, after comparing a dozen classic as well as offbeat recipes and recognizing that the years have transformed this feisty country bread into a wimpy city cake, we've come up with one we think worthy of its name. We like it best warmed for breakfast, spread with soft butter, and savored with a mug of cafe latte. It's also terrific for dessert with a big scoop of coffee or toffee ice cream.

*Serves 8*

¼ pound (1 stick) butter at room temperature

½ cup packed dark brown sugar

½ cup dark molasses, preferably Sucanat unsulphured blackstrap

2 large eggs

2 cups sifted flour

½ teaspoon baking soda

2 teaspoons ground cinnamon

1 tablespoon ground ginger

1 teaspoon freshly ground white pepper (optional)

2 teaspoons Dutch process cocoa

½ teaspoon salt

¼ cup sour cream

1 cup buttermilk

Preheat the oven to 350°. Butter and flour a 9-inch square cake pan, preferably with a removable bottom. Cream the butter using a mixer with whisking beaters, not a paddle, then add the sugar and continue creaming until the mixture is light and fluffy. Add the molasses and beat in thoroughly. Add the eggs one at a time, mixing well after each addition. Sift the flour with the rest of the dry ingredients and add in 4 parts to the creamed butter and sugar alternately with the sour cream and buttermilk, beating in slowly but thoroughly after each addition. The batter should be silky and soft, like a creamy frosting. If you're an inveterate bowl licker, this is the one.

Turn the batter into the cake pan and bake for 40 to 45 minutes or until a cake tester or a toothpick inserted in the middle comes out clean. Let the cake cool in the pan on a rack, then cover it well.

➣ *Gingerbread seems to improve in both texture and flavor if it's stored, re-warmed, and served the next day. If you can't wait, at least save some to see what we mean.*

➣ *True ginger devotees should add 2 or 3 tablespoons minced preserved or crystallized ginger to the batter, reducing the sugar by 1 or 2 tablespoons to compensate.*

➣ *Adding cocoa brings out another level of flavor but mainly it deepens the richness of color. Powdered instant coffee will accomplish the same thing.*

➣ *You can use bacon fat in place of the butter or try half butter and half bacon fat and omit the sour cream. This would be particularly tasty for a brunch cake. Use instant coffee instead of cocoa.*

➣ *For a Portuguese version of gingerbread, add 2 tablespoons Madeira to the buttermilk and omit the sour cream.*

➣ *To dress up gingerbread for a company dinner, make a center filling and topping by sautéing coarsely grated apples with a jigger of calvados or dark rum and minced preserved ginger. When cool, fill the split cake first with the apple-ginger mixture and then "ice" it with stiffly beaten whipped cream.*

# Chocolate Cake

This wonderfully moist, intensely chocolatey cake is a snap to make and it just gets better the longer it keeps. This is the sort of chocolate cake Dorothy might have been wishing her Auntie Em would make in *The Wizard of Oz*. It's based on a treasured recipe from Virginia Green, a ranch cook in West Texas, whose original recipe is served at the Liberty Bar in San Antonio, one of our favorite restaurants on the planet. You can make the frosting a day ahead, and if you have a large food processor you can make the entire cake in it. (Be sure to make the frosting at least several hours ahead.) We use regular flour here instead of cake flour; to us those perfect airy birthday cakes lack personality and don't have the nostalgic quality that makes this simple cake so, well, sexy.

*Serves 12*

### The Frosting:

12 tablespoons (1½ sticks) butter

1½ cups sugar

1½ cups heavy cream

8 ounces unsweetened baking
chocolate

1 tablespoon pure vanilla extract

### The Cake:

2 cups flour

¼ teaspoon salt

1 cup plus 3 scant tablespoons
unsweetened cocoa (Hershey's
is fine)

1 cup boiling water

1 teaspoon baking soda

3 large eggs at room temperature

2 cups sugar

12 tablespoons (1½ sticks) butter at
room temperature

1 cup buttermilk at room temperature

1 teaspoon pure vanilla extract

*190*

Cut the butter for the frosting into 1-inch cubes and refrigerate.

In a large saucepan, mix the sugar and cream. Bring to a boil over high heat and boil vigorously for 6 minutes without stirring. Remove the pan from the heat and add the chocolate, vanilla, and cold butter. Stir with a wooden spoon until combined thoroughly; be sure the chocolate is completely melted. Refrigerate for 1 hour. Remove from the refrigerator and beat well before spreading on the cake.

Preheat the oven to 350°. Grease two 9-inch nonstick cake pans with vegetable shortening and flour them.

Sift the flour into a mixing bowl and add the baking powder and salt; whisk to mix together and set aside.

Sift the cocoa and place in a 2-cup glass measure. Add the boiling water and mix well, stirring up the dry cocoa at the bottom. When the cocoa is dissolved, add the baking soda, but don't stir it in. Set aside.

Place the eggs and sugar in a food processor fitted with the metal blade. Blend for 1 minute. Stop, scrape down the sides, and blend for 30 seconds more. Add the butter, blend for 1 minute, and scrape the sides again. Blend for 30 seconds more. Add the buttermilk and vanilla. Pulse 3 or 4 times and scrape down. Pulse again. Add the cocoa mixture and pulse 3 times. Scrape down and pulse once.

If the work bowl is full at this point, pour the mixture into a mixing bowl and add the flour mixture, mixing by hand until smooth. If you have room in the food processor, add the flour, pulse 3 times, and scrape down. Pulse once more.

---

### Snow Ice Cream

*No treat from city sidewalks, to be sure, but where the snow is pure and driven, have some delightful family fun with snow ice cream. Beat 3 large eggs with 2 cups half-and-half. Add 1 cup confectioners' sugar, 1 tablespoon pure vanilla extract, and several gratings of nutmeg. Pour the mixture over 4 quarts of packed snow piled in a deep bowl and fold until blended. Dig in immediately. Try adding cocoa or espresso powder instead of nutmeg or simply mix in ready-made eggnog, usually available as the snow lies all around.*

Pour the batter equally into the prepared pans. Rap them sharply on the counter to eliminate any air bubbles and put them in the oven for 35 minutes or until a tooth-pick inserted in the center comes out dry.

When the cakes are done, remove them from the oven and let them stand for 2 minutes, then invert them over wire racks and turn out the cakes. Let the cakes cool completely before frosting.

 *If the sugared milk for the frosting threatens to boil over, you can lower the heat a little, but continue to keep it at a boil.*

 EVEN EASIER FROSTING: *Melt one 12-ounce package of semisweet chocolate chips in the microwave; stir every 15 seconds. Gradually stir in 2 cups sour cream, a few tablespoons at a time. When the mixture is completely smooth, refrigerate for 30 minutes or until thick enough to spread. Drag the tines of a fork across the frosting in an interesting pattern to decorate.*

# Mississippi Mud Cake

This first cousin to a brownie is the dessert to make when you need one fast. The whole cake is made in a saucepan, and you can frost it or not, as you like. Your cake will be ready in an hour, and your guests will be extremely happy—mud cake simply vanishes. You can also spread the unfrosted cake with softened coffee ice cream, top with sweetened whipped cream, and freeze the whole thing. Gild the lily with chocolate sauce when you serve it.

*Serves 10*

½ pound (2 sticks) butter

½ cup unsweetened cocoa
  (Hershey's is fine)

2 cups sugar

4 large eggs, lightly beaten

1½ cups flour

1 teaspoon baking powder

1½ cups chopped pecans

1 teaspoon pure vanilla extract

pinch of salt

**The Frosting:**

1 16-ounce box confectioners' sugar,
  sifted

½ cup milk

⅓ cup unsweetened cocoa

4 tablespoons (½ stick) butter,
  softened to room temperature

Preheat the oven to 350°. Butter an 8- by 10-inch Pyrex pan.

In a large saucepan, melt the butter and cocoa together over low heat. Off the heat, stir in the sugar and eggs and mix well. Add everything else and mix well.

Pour into the prepared pan and bake for 35 to 45 minutes. Remove from the oven and cool on a rack. When the cake is cool, frost it. To make the frosting, mix the ingredients together well in a bowl and spread over the top of the cake. When the frosting hardens, cut the cake into squares and serve with vanilla ice cream.

# Brownies

There's hardly a cookbook published in America these days that doesn't have a brownie recipe, and of course there are entire books devoted to brownies.

We think the best brownies are made with chocolate, not cocoa—so there's an extra little step here of melting the chocolate and butter. They're both chewy and moist: Beneath the crunchy exterior lies a bed of unctuous rich chocolate.

*Makes 36 brownies*

4 ounces unsweetened chocolate

¼ pound (1 stick) butter

4 large eggs at room temperature,
    beaten until light

big pinch of salt

2 cups sugar

2 teaspoons pure vanilla extract

1 cup flour

1 cup pecan or walnut pieces

Preheat the oven to 350°. Butter a 9- by 13-inch Pyrex baking dish.

Melt the chocolate with the butter in a heavy saucepan over low heat. Or do it in the microwave, checking every 15 seconds and giving it a stir to be sure it's not burning. The chocolate will be melted before it looks melted. Set aside to cool.

Beat the eggs with the salt, then slowly add the sugar and vanilla. When the chocolate-butter mixture has cooled, add it to the eggs and sugar and mix briefly to combine. Add the flour, then the nuts, mix briefly again, and pour into the prepared pan. Bake for 25 minutes, then cool on a rack.

For clean-cut brownies with no ragged edges, chill the pan for an hour before you cut them. Wrap the brownies individually in plastic wrap or foil to store for a few days.

*Try shredded coconut instead of nuts.*

*Keys to success: don't overmix, don't overbake, and keep overnight before cutting, if you can stand to.*

*Milk is the classic accompaniment, but a scoop of vanilla ice cream is great with brownies too.*

# Blondies

We forget about these from year to year, but everyone loves them, so try making a batch. The flavor is butterscotch; if you're serving brownies for dessert, mix in some blondies for a big treat.

### *Makes about 36 blondies*

¼ pound (1 stick) butter

2 cups packed light brown sugar

2 large eggs

2 teaspoons pure vanilla extract

1 cup flour

1½ teaspoons baking powder

½ teaspoon salt

1 cup chopped walnuts

Preheat the oven to 350°. Butter a 9- by 13-inch Pyrex baking dish.

In a heavy saucepan, melt the butter over low heat and stir in the brown sugar until it dissolves. Set aside to cool.

When it's cool, add the eggs and vanilla to the saucepan and beat in well. Stir in the flour, baking powder, and salt, then add the nuts. Pour into the prepared pan and bake for 25 minutes. Cool on a rack before cutting.

# Fruit Cobbler

This mindless dish is the one to turn to for dessert when you have good local fruit on hand—berries, apricots, peaches. The batter rises mysteriously to the top, even though it goes in on the bottom of the pan.

*Serves 4*

4 tablespoons (½ stick) butter
½ cup flour
½ cup sugar

1 teaspoon baking powder
½ cup milk
2 cups sweetened fruit

Preheat the oven to 350°. Put the butter in a baking dish—about an 8-inch square—and melt it in the oven. Mix together the flour, sugar, baking powder, and milk. Pour the batter over the melted butter and cover it with the fruit. Bake for about an hour or until the top is golden brown. Serve hot, warm, or at room temperature with heavy cream or vanilla ice cream.

➣ *You can easily double this recipe.*

➣ *Pure and simple as it is, this dish can also take a little extra flavoring— a little cinnamon with blueberries, a little grated lemon zest with blackberries, etc.*

➣ *Biscuit dough (page 167) works just fine as a cobbler topping. Add a tablespoon of sugar to the biscuit dough and spread it on top of the fruit. Bake at 450° for about 20 minutes or until golden brown.*

➣ *In the same ballpark is another kind of cobbler, the slump. It's not as rich, and it's flavored with vanilla.*

# Berry Slump

*Serves 6*

| | |
|---|---|
| 4 cups berries | pinch of salt |
| 1 cup sugar | ¼ cup milk |
| 1 cup flour | 2 tablespoons butter |
| 1½ teaspoons baking powder | ½ teaspoon pure vanilla extract |

Preheat the oven to 375°. Butter a baking dish about 9 inches wide. Mix the berries with three quarters of the sugar and put them in the prepared dish. Mix together the remaining sugar, flour, baking powder, and salt. Warm the milk (the microwave will work) and melt the butter in it. Add the milk to the flour mixture along with the vanilla. Spread the batter over the berries and bake for 45 minutes or until golden brown. Serve warm.

## *Bananas Foster*

*For each serving, cut 1 medium-ripe banana in half lengthwise. In a nonstick skillet over high heat, melt ½ tablespoon butter with 1½ tablespoons dark brown sugar and a little pinch of salt until the mixture starts to bubble. Lay in the banana halves, reduce the heat to medium, and continue to caramelize the sugar and cook the banana. When the sugar and butter are syrupy, add ¼ teaspoon pure vanilla extract and 1 tablespoon dark rum. Ignite the rum and carefully transfer the banana to a serving plate. Serve with a scoop of vanilla ice cream.*

# Piecrust

*E*ven a generation ago, almost every American family had at least one piecrust genius who could turn out a delectable, flaky, melt-in-your-mouth pastry in nothing flat. Today even many otherwise accomplished cooks quail at the thought of making a pie. But we're still crazy about pie, and since no one's invented a piecrust machine for our kitchens, it's worth making a few pies to get your confidence up—then you too can think nothing of rolling out a piecrust on a moment's notice.

To make a delicious, tender, flaky crust, here's what you need to know:

THE FAT: Butter will give you a delicious crust that's slightly hard; real lard (from a butcher) gives a tasty crust with wonderful flakes; vegetable shortening gives the flakiest crust of all with virtually no flavor. In the absence of real lard, which is hard to come by, we vote for a mix of butter and vegetable shortening, leaning a little more toward butter for better flavor. (Oil doesn't make good piecrusts.)

THE LIQUID: Water, specifically ice water, and as little of it as possible—too much and you lose the flakes and tenderness.

SUGAR: You don't actually need sugar at all, even for sweet pies, but you may want a little sweetness, and sugar also helps the crust brown (to help brown the lower crust, butter the pie plate before putting the crust in).

THE METHOD: The easiest way is the food processor. Second easiest is using a pastry cutter, an inexpensive gizmo that's basically just a handle with four looped wires attached. Once you get a feel for the dough, you'll be able to use your fingers.

TEMPERATURE: It's crucial to keep everything as cold as possible so the fat doesn't melt until it's in the oven. Chill the fats (or freeze them if you're using a food processor). You can even chill the dough up to 24 hours before you roll it out. Try not to touch the dough with your hands any more than necessary—use only your fingers and rinse them first in cold water. Be speedy: Cut the fats in quickly, add the liquid quickly, and roll out quickly; otherwise your pastry will toughen up right away.

 ROLLING OUT WITH A LIGHT HAND: Air is an ingredient in pastry too, so you want to roll the dough out lightly. The best no-fuss way to deal with rolling out the crust is so good that we're giving no other directions. It's based on a tip from Mayumi Akiyoshi of Chicago, who sent it in to share with *Cook's Illustrated* readers. Get your hands on some 2-gallon heavy-duty freezer plastic zipper-lock bags (the lighter storage bags will tangle up and the 1-gallon size is too small for a 9-inch pie). When you chill the dough before rolling it out, stick it right in the bag, in which you will also roll out the crust.

 TOOLS: Pyrex pie pan, rolling pin with ball bearing handles, pastry brush for brushing on a glaze.

 KEY POINTS: Keep it cold, work fast, handle the dough as little as possible—and remember, even if it's not perfect, your homemade piecrust will taste delicious.

*Makes 2 piecrusts*

3 cups flour, poured into a bowl, then
  scooped into measuring cups and
  leveled off with a knife
1 teaspoon salt

2 teaspoons sugar (optional)
1 cup chilled fat in small bits
½ cup ice water plus 3 tablespoons in
  a separate container

Have everything you need ready to go—if you're using a food processor, freeze the fats first. If you're using the pastry cutter, cut the chilled fat into thin flakes the thickness of a quarter. Have two 2-gallon heavy-duty zipper-lock plastic bags ready to receive the dough for chilling.

### Food Processor Method:

Put the flour, salt, and sugar in the work bowl fitted with the steel blade. Process for 10 seconds to blend. Remove the cover and add the chilled bits of fat. Spoon some of the flour over them. Replace the cover and process in quick on-off pulses—not more than 10 pulses—until you have what looks like coarse cornmeal. Remove the cover and add ¼ cup of the ice water, pouring it in around the edges of the bowl. Replace the cover and pulse 2 more times.

Now add ice water through the tube a bit at a time, pulsing on and off until the dough starts to mass up—it will still look crumbly but not dry. Try not to use all of the ½ cup of ice water (though you may have to use more, which is why you have the 3 tablespoons). If the dough jumps on top of the blade in a ball, you've gone too far and the pastry will be tough. It's just right when you pinch it between your fingers and it sticks together.

Form the dough into two 5-inch disks, one slightly larger for the bottom crust, and place them inside the plastic bags. Refrigerate them for 30 minutes before rolling out. You can roll the dough out right away if you need to.

### Pastry Cutter Method:

Put the flour, salt, and sugar in a stainless-steel or aluminum bowl—you can chill it first if it's a hot day—and mix it to blend with a wire whisk. Add two thirds of the fat slivers and spoon some flour over them to cover. Working quickly, cut the fat into the flour with the pastry cutter by bringing it forward against the front of the bowl, then moving it over the mixture and back down through it in a circular motion. With your other hand, turn the bowl continuously so that you're reaching all the flour mixture. When you have what looks like coarse cornmeal, add the rest of the fat and cut it in until it looks like peas.

Sprinkle ¼ cup of the ice water over the mixture and mix it in gently with a rubber spatula. Add more water by the tablespoon as needed, stopping right away when the dough begins to hold together—pinch it between your fingers; if it sticks together, it's done. Form the dough into two 5-inch disks, one slightly larger than the other for the bottom crust, and place them inside the plastic bags. Refrigerate them for 30 minutes before rolling out.

## Rolling Out:

Have everything ready: Have the oven preheated and the filling ready if the pie is going in now, have the pan to hand, buttered if you like. Have ready the rolling pin and the pastry brush. The flour should be within easy reach in case you need it—the dough may stick to the bag.

Put the larger pastry disk (which should be exactly in the center of the plastic bag) on the work surface and start to roll it out, using a light touch, from the center to the edge. If it seems too stiff, let it rest for about 5 minutes—or up to 30 minutes if it's really cold—and begin again. Keep rolling around in a circle, lightening up as you near the edge, which will otherwise get too thin. Lift and turn the entire bag as you work your way around the circle. Continue to roll evenly until you have a circle that's about 2 to 3 inches larger than the pie plate. The dough should be about ⅛ inch thick.

Cut apart 2 sides of the bag with scissors and open it like a book. If the pastry is cracked, press it together lightly with your fingers; if it's broken, harvest a piece from the outer edge and patch the hole; replace the top layer of the bag and roll over it.

Place the pastry directly over the pie plate and peel away the bag. Lift the crust gently at the outer edge and fit it loosely into the plate, being careful not to stretch it. Using a sharp knife, cut away the excess dough, which can be used to cut out decorations for the pie if you're so inclined—try not to roll it again. Brush the rim of the bottom crust with a little water or milk to help seal the two crusts together.

If you're making a juicy pie, brush some melted butter over the bottom crust so it won't get soggy. A little beaten egg white works, too—let it dry before you add the filling.

For the top crust, repeat the procedure, but cut an extra ½-inch overlap for the edge of the crust. Fold the excess under and crimp the 2 crusts together with the tines of a fork. Cut at least 4 steam holes in a decorative pattern in the top crust. Brush with egg wash—an egg beaten with 2 tablespoons water—to make a glaze. Sprinkle with sugar for a sparkly top crust.

To prebake a crust, set the oven to 425°. Put the crust in the pie pan and prick with a fork in several places. Freeze the pan for 10 minutes, then bake about 20 minutes, until lightly brown. Cool on a rack.

~ *For extra insurance on flakiness and tenderness, refrigerate the crust in the pan for 30 minutes before baking.*

~ *You can freeze either the disks of pastry dough, well wrapped, or the rolled-out crusts inside their plastic bags—though they're a bit fragile, and they'll be a little less flaky and tougher than fresh-made pastry.*

~ *It's easier to measure lard if it's softened to room temperature first. If it's in a block, it's easy to measure by cutting a stick the size of butter, and slicing off tablespoons by the ½ inch. If you're mixing fats, mix them at room temperature and then chill them or freeze them. If you get your hands on some good lard, freeze it in ½-cup portions so it's ready to use.*

~ *Fill the pie at the last minute before you bake it. If the crust needs to wait, cover it with plastic wrap and refrigerate it after it's rolled.*

~ *Of course you can flavor piecrusts, with spices, citrus zest, grated cheese, etc. Just toss together with the dry ingredients.*

~ *If you're baking the pie on a baking sheet, put it in the oven while it's preheating—a cold baking sheet will affect the bottom crust.*

~ *Cool all pies on a wire rack.*

~ *Pies are best a few hours after they're baked; they don't keep well.*

# Apple Pie

he classic of all classics, aka Mom's apple pie, mile-high apple pie, country apple pie. The time to make this pie is late summer and fall, when the new apple crop comes in—that's when Paula Reds, Winesaps, Gravensteins, Northern Spies, and other nice tart crisp apples come into the market, especially the farmers' market. You can also use Granny Smiths and make the pie at any time of year, of course.

*Serves 6*

2½ pounds tart apples, cored, peeled, and sliced (not too thin), about 5 cups

½ cup granulated sugar

2 tablespoons packed light brown sugar

fresh lemon juice to taste, plus grated zest (optional)

several pinches of freshly grated nutmeg

several pinches of ground cinnamon

2 teaspoons rice flour (available at natural foods stores, or grind rice to a powder in a spice mill) or potato starch

1 piecrust (page 198)

2 tablespoons butter, cut into bits

Preheat the oven to 400°.

In a large bowl, mix the apple slices gently with the sugars, lemon juice (just a splash if the apples are tart; more as well as some lemon zest if they're not), spices, and flour. Set aside for 15 minutes or until you're ready to bake the pie.

Arrange the rolled piecrust in a 9-inch Pyrex pan. When you're ready to bake the pie, fill it with the apples, mounding them up in the center and fitting them carefully together. Spoon any leftover liquid from the apples over them. Distribute the bits of butter evenly over the apples.

Cover the apples with the top crust, leaving an extra ½-inch overhang to tuck under around the edges. Cut at least 4 steam vents into the top crust. Crimp the edges of the pie with the tines of a fork.

Bake in the lower third of the oven for 30 minutes or until light brown. Lower the temperature to 350° and continue baking for 30 minutes or until the pie is golden brown. Test the apples with a knife point through one of the vents to be sure they're soft.

Cool the pie on a wire rack for at least 1 hour and serve with vanilla ice cream.

*The easiest way to deal with the apples is to peel them, then use one of those gadgets that cores and slices them simultaneously.*

*Since you're going to all this trouble, you might opt for a little more effort to get a professional-looking pie: a sparkly glaze. With a pastry brush, cover the top crust (but not the edges) with milk or beaten egg white—but don't let it collect in the valleys of the crust; soak it up with paper towels if it pools. Then sprinkle the crust with a little sugar.*

### Truffles

*Here's a quick, delicious version of a perennial favorite. In a small microwave-safe bowl, melt 1 cup chopped semisweet chocolate with 2 tablespoons butter. Zap the chocolate at 1½-minute intervals and test to see if it's soft—it will hold the shape of the chunks; if it liquefies, it will be scorched. Stir the chocolate vigorously until it regains its gloss. Quickly whisk in ¼ cup heavy cream and 3 tablespoons of Kahlúa or a liqueur of your choice. Cover and chill until firm enough to roll into small balls. Roll each ball in a mixture of two thirds cocoa, one third confectioners' sugar, and espresso powder to taste if you use Kahlúa. Chill. Try brandy, peppermint, hot cinnamon, or coconut liqueur for alternate flavors. Roll in nut powder, fine cookie crumbs, or toasted coconut.*

*Rice flour gives you the least pasty thickening for the apples, but you can also use cornstarch or tapioca or even flour.*

*The easiest apple tart is from the brilliant chef Jean-Georges Vongerichten: Stack four 6-inch rounds of phyllo dough (in the freezer at the supermarket) and paint the top one with 1 tablespoon melted butter. Bake on a baking sheet at 400° on the lowest oven rack for 5 minutes. Place thin slices from a big apple in a spiral over the phyllo, starting at the edge and overlapping as you go toward the center. Drizzle 2 tablespoons melted butter over the apples and sprinkle on a tablespoon of sugar. Bake for 15 minutes and serve hot.*

# Lemon Meringue Pie

This is arguably one of the great American culinary contributions—there are brilliant lemon tarts in France, yes, but the airy meringue combined with the sweet, rich tart filling is something else altogether, a sensational dessert.

Meringue can be tricky, especially if the weather is humid (a time you'd particularly like to see refreshing meringue pie). But pay attention to the directions and you won't have problems. If handling egg whites seems like too much, just make the simple lemon tart at the end of the recipe.

*Serves 8*

Prebaked 9-inch single piecrust (page 198) or cookie crumb crust (see notes below)

1 large egg white, beaten, for pastry crust

**The Filling:**

1½ cups sugar

3 heaped tablespoons cornstarch

pinch of salt

1½ cups water

4 large egg yolks, lightly beaten

½ cup fresh lemon juice

3 tablespoons butter

2 tablespoons grated lemon zest
  (optional)

**The Meringue:**

4 large egg whites at room
  temperature

¼ teaspoon cream of tartar

½ cup superfine sugar

½ teaspoon pure vanilla extract

Once you have your piecrust, chill it in the refrigerator or freezer. Preheat the oven to 350°, line the crust with foil, and add some dry beans to weight it down. Bake for 10 minutes, remove the beans, then bake for another 10 minutes. Remove to a rack to cool. Or make a cookie crumb crust, as directed in the notes at the end of the recipe.

For the filling, combine the sugar, cornstarch, and salt in a medium saucepan. Add the water gradually, stirring constantly. Over medium heat, cook and stir constantly with a whisk until the mixture thickens and comes to a boil. Immediately remove from the heat and add a third of the hot mixture to the egg yolks. Mix well and add the egg yolk mixture to the saucepan. Cook, stirring constantly, over low heat for 2 minutes. Stir in the remaining filling ingredients and set the filling aside, covered. You'll reheat it before baking it. Now make the meringue.

Preheat the oven to 325°. Put the egg whites in the bowl of a mixer and sprinkle the cream of tartar over them. Beat at high speed until you have soft peaks. Beat in the sugar a tablespoon at a time. Beat until all the sugar is dissolved and you have stiff glossy peaks. Beat in the vanilla.

Reheat the filling over low heat and pour it into the pie shell. Spread the meringue over the pie with a rubber spatula, swirling it into attractive swoops. Be generous with the meringue at the edges, covering the pie completely and sealing it to the edge of the pie shell. Bake the pie for 20 minutes, until the meringue is browned lightly. Cool on a rack for about 2 hours or until it reaches room temperature before serving.

     &#10148; *Separating the eggs: Do this while they're cold. If this process makes you anxious, use a funnel over a glass measure. Crack the egg into the funnel; the yolk will stay in, and the white will run down into the cup. Be sure no egg yolk reaches the whites or they won't beat up to their full volume. Let the eggs reach room temperature before you proceed.*

     &#10148; *Gingersnap or graham cracker crust: You'll need 2 cups of crumbs. Put the broken cookies in a food processor. In a bowl, add ¼ pound (1 stick) melted butter to the crumbs along with 3 tablespoons packed light brown sugar and a pinch of salt. Mix together with a fork. Smear a 9-inch pie pan with soft butter and press the cookie crust over it to cover evenly. Preheat the oven to 325°. Chill the pie shell for at least 15 minutes, in the refrigerator or the freezer, then bake for 10 minutes. Let cool before filling.*

     &#10148; *Make your own superfine sugar by whirling regular sugar in a food processor or blender.*

     &#10148; *If it's a rainy day, try this tip from the tireless folks at Cook's magazine, which they guarantee will stop your meringue from weeping: Before you start the meringue, mix 1 tablespoon cornstarch with ⅓ cup water in a small saucepan. Bring it to a simmer over medium heat, whisking. When it simmers and turns clear, remove from heat and let cool while you start the meringue. Add the cornstarch mixture at the soft peak stage of beating the meringue, and beat it in 1 tablespoon at a time.*

     &#10148; *For the meringue, try using powdered egg whites—Just Whites, at the supermarket.*

     &#10148; *If all this fuss seems completely overwhelming, try this simple lemon tart instead: Have ready a prebaked 8-inch pie shell. Remove the zest from 1 lemon and put it in a food processor along with 1¼ cups sugar. Pulse several times to flavor the sugar. Add 4 large eggs and process for 1 minute, scraping down the sides at the end. Add the juice of 4 lemons and 4 tablespoons unsalted butter, melted. Pulse to blend, then pour into the pie shell. Bake at 350° for 25 minutes or until the pie is set. Let cool on a rack before serving.*

# Pecan Pie

This is the pie to take if someone insists you bring a pie somewhere—Thanksgiving dinner, for instance. Once you have the crust (and although we hope you made it yourself, we realize that you might have acquired it) it takes 3 minutes to put this pie together. Some people sigh and complain that it's too rich, too sweet, or they don't ever eat dessert, but they always eat it all. Serve skinny slices; it's truly rich.

*Serves 10*

1 piecrust (page 198)

3 large eggs, lightly beaten

½ cup light corn syrup

4 tablespoons (½ stick) butter, melted

pinch of salt

1 cup packed dark brown sugar

2 teaspoons pure vanilla extract

1½ cups pecan halves, about 1
    pound, roughly cut (save a handful
    of whole ones to decorate the top
    of the pie) and toasted

Preheat the oven to 400°. Fit the crust into a 9-inch deep dish Pyrex pie plate. Crimp the edges with the tines of a fork.

Mix everything but the pecans together well, then stir in the nuts and pour the filling into the piecrust. Scatter the reserved pecan halves on top decoratively.

## Baking Tips

As a general rule, have everything at room temperature. If you forget to take the eggs out of the refrigerator, just submerge them in a bowl of warm water for a few minutes before cracking them.

To measure flour, use the dip-and-sweep method: Stir the flour to lighten it, then scoop it over the measuring cup, letting it fall in. Level the top with the straight edge of a knife.

If separating eggs makes you nervous, do it in a funnel placed over a 2-cup glass measure. Crack the whole egg into the funnel—the yolk stays in the funnel, and the white runs through into the cup below. Cold eggs are easiest to separate, but do it ahead so the eggs will be at room temperature when you're ready to use them.

You can make your own superfine sugar by whirling it in a food processor briefly. Use this sugar for cakes.

The easiest way to grease cake pans is with vegetable shortening, which is also less likely to stick than butter.

To keep cookies from sticking to the pan—and to avoid washing the cookie sheet—use parchment paper (in some supermarkets or the hardware store) or lightweight aluminum foil—heavy-duty foil won't work.

Melt chocolate carefully in the microwave. Check and stir every 15 seconds; the chocolate will be melted before it looks melted.

If you have a baking stone, use it for baking pies—just set the pie plate directly on the baking stone in the oven, and the bottom crust will brown much better.

Contrary to popular wisdom, bleached flour is usually best for baking—piecrusts, cookies, quick breads, pancakes, even pound cake work better with bleached flour.

Southern cook Edna Lewis claims that you should keep cookie dough in the refrigerator a day before baking the cookies, and they'll have better flavor and texture. We think she's right.

> *Instead of weighting your pie shell with beans to partially bake it, try using loose change—the extra heat from the metal will help the crust to bake more evenly. And be sure you're not using heavy-duty foil to hold the coins; you'll get a sodden crust that way. Better yet, use our prebaking method on page 202 for a no-fuss alternative.*
>
> *You can't overbeat cake batter until the flour goes in; once it does, be quick and get it in the oven fast.*
>
> *If the weather is very damp, dry the flour before you measure it. Spread it out on a sheet pan and set it in a 200° oven for 30 minutes.*

Bake for 15 minutes, then lower the heat to 350° and bake for 45 minutes. If it looks like the crust is getting too dark, cover it with a strip of foil. Transfer the pie to a rack to cool.

🍃 *You might want to add a spoonful of cider vinegar to cut the sweetness.*

🍃 *You can also add a little espresso or a handful of coconut to the filling.*

## Peach Melba

*Once again—and, we think, evermore—this is a stylish dessert. Never mind the original Lohengrin swan ice sculpture version with vanilla syrup invented by Escoffier to honor Australian diva Nellie Melba at the Savoy. Just present a sparkling crystal compote holding a blushing, ripe peach half filled with vanilla bean ice cream, drizzled with brilliant raspberry puree, and garnished with crystallized violets or a sprig of mint. When fresh raspberries are plentiful, we process them with a little framboise and superfine sugar and remove the seeds by pushing the mixture through a strainer with the back of a wooden spoon. That's about all the work there is except peeling the peaches, and the puree can always be in the freezer, since frozen raspberries work perfectly.*

## Rice Pudding

This recipe comes from the brilliant British food writer Jane Grigson, who had a wonderful understanding of simple food, expertly prepared. Rice pudding has both British and Spanish origins; it's the essence of nursery food. Grigson's rice pudding is simplicity itself; in fact, you have to choose between the vanilla bean and the cinnamon stick—both would be complicating the flavor too much. The key to her method is using the right rice and a very low oven temperature, the lower the better, for long slow cooking. It seems like too little rice, but it isn't.

*Serves 4*

scant ½ cup short-grain rice, Arborio
   or other rice for risotto
4 to 5 cups milk, plus a little cream
   (optional)

2 tablespoons butter
2 tablespoons sugar
1 split vanilla bean or 1 cinnamon
   stick

Preheat the oven to 275°. Mix all the ingredients (but only half the milk) together and put them in a heatproof ceramic or glass dish. Bake for 3 hours, stirring up the rice and adding more milk to loosen the mixture after 1 hour. After 2 hours, do it again and perhaps add some cream as well.

At the end of the cooking, a delicious skin will have formed on top of the pudding. Remove the vanilla bean or cinnamon stick and serve warm or cold with cream.

↪ *At 225°, you can cook the pudding twice as long and persuade it to absorb even more milk, another cup or so.*

↪ *No one's stopping you from adding a little grated nutmeg, some raisins, some lemon or orange zest, or any of the other things people like to put in rice pudding—but try it this way first.*

# Baked Custard

This delectable but incredibly simple dessert is real comfort food. You can dress it up with caramel and bake it in a mold for company—see the notes at the end of the recipe. The water bath is a snap and guarantees you a silky smooth custard.

Although it's made with milk and not cream, this custard tastes especially rich because it has extra egg yolks. And it's made in a blender, so you can put it together in seconds.

*Serves 4*

2 cups scalded milk (heated to just
    the point when tiny bubbles
    appear)
4 large eggs plus 3 egg yolks
½ cup sugar

2 teaspoons pure vanilla extract or
    more to taste
freshly grated nutmeg for garnish
    (optional)

Preheat the oven to 350°. Have ready a 2-quart soufflé dish or ovenproof glass bowl that will fit inside a larger shallow pan, such as a roasting pan.

Pour the hot milk into a blender jar and add the eggs, sugar, and vanilla. Blend well. With a spoon, skim off the froth at the top of the jar and pour the custard into the baking dish. Dust with the nutmeg if you're using it. Set the dish inside the larger pan and put it in the oven. Add hot water to the larger pan to come 1 inch up the side of the baking dish.

Bake for 30 minutes or until the color begins to change. Test with a straw a couple of inches in from the side of the dish; when the straw comes out clean, the custard is ready. (The center will still be jiggly in any case.)

Let the custard cool on a rack. Serve warm or cover and refrigerate until ready to serve.

If you're in a rush, you don't really have to scald the milk, but it does make the custard smoother.

A teaspoon of pure vanilla extract is just the beginning for us; we love it so much that even a tablespoon doesn't seem too much. A top-quality vanilla extract—Neilsen-Massey or Cook's—will shine here, but it's a luxury.

Other flavoring options: a tablespoon of dark rum, a teaspoon of almond extract, maple syrup substituted for the sugar.

You can bake the custard in individual cups or ramekins, and you can also bake it in the water bath in the microwave—about 5 minutes on MEDIUM for 4 cups of custard.

BAKED CUSTARD WITH CARAMEL SAUCE:  In a heavy skillet (cast iron is perfect), heat ½ cup sugar until it begins to caramelize, stirring with a wooden spoon. You can stop this process at any point, depending on how strong you want the sugar sauce to taste—if you let it go until it's dark, you'll have a burned sugar taste, which some people love. The minute the caramel is done, pour it into the baking dish or an ovenproof mold and roll it all around so that it coats the sides and bottom of the dish. Proceed with the custard recipe. Once the cooked custard has chilled thoroughly, unmold it by placing it in 3 inches of hot water for a minute. Gently pry the sides loose with a thin-bladed knife and invert the custard onto a plate with a rim to contain the caramel sauce. Spoon a little extra sauce over each serving.

# Crème Brûlée

*I*f custard is homey and comforting, crème brûlée is elegant and so sexy it's irresistible, with its rich silken interior hiding under a crackling burned sugar skin. The translation—broiled cream—of this Creole dish hardly does it justice. The broiling part scared off home cooks for many years because they were advised to use an expensive gadget called a salamander heated red-hot to melt the sugar. Savvy cooks now use a propane torch, but you can use the broiler too—it just takes a little careful watching to be sure the sugar doesn't actually burn.

Best of all, you can make the custard a day ahead and just caramelize the sugar a few minutes before you serve it.

*Serves 6*

| | |
|---|---|
| 5 large eggs | 1 cup heavy cream |
| 4 egg yolks | 1 teaspoon pure vanilla extract or |
| ½ cup sugar |     more to taste |
| 3 cups half-and-half | ¼ cup packed light brown sugar |

Preheat the oven to 325°. Have ready a 1½-quart flameproof shallow baking dish that will fit snugly inside a larger shallow pan or ovenproof skillet.

In a blender jar, combine everything but the brown sugar and blend well. Skim off the froth with a spoon and pour the custard into the baking dish. Put the filled baking dish inside the larger pan in the middle of the oven. Add hot water to come halfway up the side of the baking dish. Bake for 40 minutes or until a tester inserted close to the edge comes out clean.

Let the custard cool completely on a rack. Cover and chill for at least 3 hours or overnight.

To caramelize the custard, use a strainer to sift the brown sugar evenly over the top. Use a propane torch with automatic ignition to melt the sugar. The torches are inexpensive at the hardware store. To use one, wave it back and forth a few inches above the custard. Or light the broiler and place the baking dish about 6 inches from the heat. Broil for 2 or 3 minutes, until the sugar is melted; turn the dish several times and watch carefully to be sure the sugar's not getting burned. Chill for 10 minutes before serving.

> *This dish is so pure it doesn't need gilding, but we do love gingered crème brûlée. Just mince a few tablespoons of candied ginger and stir them into the custard before it goes into the oven.*

> *If you have a really good vanilla bean on your shelf, here's the place to use it, in addition to the vanilla extract. Place the cream and half-and-half in a small saucepan. Scrape the seeds from the slit bean into the cream and half-and-half, and gently heat until the first bubble appears. Remove from heat and let steep for 5 minutes.*

## Chocolate Mousse

If you can separate eggs, you can make this mousse, which will make your guests extremely happy. Even if you can't separate eggs you can still do it using the tip that follows the recipe.

Because this mousse is so simple, it's really important to use the best-quality chocolate you can—Valrhona, Lindt, or Tobler will do fine.

*Serves 8*

½ pound bittersweet chocolate, in
  pieces

3 tablespoons orange liqueur or rum

2 teaspoons pure vanilla extract

5 large eggs, separated

¼ cup superfine sugar

Melt the chocolate in the microwave on MEDIUM with the liqueur and vanilla, checking every 20 seconds to be sure it doesn't begin to scorch—the chocolate will be melted before it loses its shape. Keep testing with a spoon to see if it's soft. Beat the chocolate with a spoon until it's entirely smooth and glossy.

Beat the egg yolks together in a bowl and, when they're light colored, add the sugar and mix well. While the chocolate is still warm, beat it into the eggs. Put the chocolate mixture into a large bowl.

Beat the egg whites until stiff. Carefully blend a third of the whites into the chocolate, then gently fold in the remaining whites with a rubber spatula, scraping down to the bottom and gently lifting up with each stroke. When there are no white streaks left, put the mousse into a large serving bowl and refrigerate, covered with plastic wrap, for at least 6 hours before serving.

  *If you can't deal with separating eggs, put a kitchen funnel over a glass measure and crack the egg into the funnel—the yolk will be caught in the fun-*

### Quick and Easy Fudge

Coat an 8-inch square pan generously with soft butter. Melt 2 cups chopped semisweet chocolate—chips are fine—in ⅔ cup evaporated milk, 1¾ cups sugar, and a pinch of salt. Bring the mixture to a boil over medium heat, stirring continuously. Simmer and stir for about 5 minutes. Remove from the heat and add ½ cup toasted nuts, beating until the chocolate is completely melted and the mixture is smooth and glossy. Pour the mixture into the pan and let cool. Cut into squares and store in an airtight container.

nel, and the white will run into the glass. Be careful not to get any yolk into the white and be sure your equipment is really clean; if there's any grease, the egg whites won't rise much.

➤ If you'd prefer the mousse without any alcohol, just skip it.

➤ Let the mousse rest out of the refrigerator while you're serving dinner— the closer it comes to room temperature, the deeper the flavor.

# Baked Apples

*I*t's hard to think of a simpler, homier dessert than this one—so down-home that it's almost disappeared from contemporary cookbooks. Make these in fall, when apples are at their best, and serve them warm with a pitcher of real heavy cream— to some tastes, this basic dish rivals apple pie.

If you don't have glorious apples, be sure to use the spices and lemon zest. Your goal here is to find a really tasty apple that will hold its shape—Cortlands, Gravensteins, Spitzenbergs, Northern Spies, Stayman Winesaps, and other farmers' market types—and to bake it long enough so that it's meltingly soft inside but still crisp on the top.

*Serves 4*

*4 baking apples*
*dash of ground cinnamon (optional)*
*dash of freshly grated nutmeg*
  *(optional)*

*grated zest of 1 lemon and a few*
  *drops of juice (optional)*
*⅓ to ½ cup sugar*

Preheat the oven to 350°. Core the apples and peel down an inch or two from the top. Set the apples in an ovenproof ceramic or glass baking dish with a low rim. If you're using the spices and lemon zest, mix them in with half the sugar in a bowl and distribute among the cored apples. Sprinkle a few drops of lemon juice into the holes if you like.

Place the dish in the oven and add ½ inch of water to the bottom. Baste the apples with the liquid in the bottom of the dish every 10 minutes. Test them after 30 minutes; they should be soft.

Raise the heat to 425°. Sprinkle the remaining sugar over the tops of the apples and bake for another 5 minutes or until the tops are golden and the sugar has turned crisp. Serve warm in bowls with some of the liquid spooned over and cream on the side, if you like.

✐ *Try using cider or apple juice instead of water.*

✐ *Of course you can stuff the cored apples with raisins, chopped nuts, chopped dates, other dried fruits, more spices, buttered bread crumbs, etc. You can use orange instead of lemon, add a little bourbon or rum to the water, add a pat of butter at the last sugaring—but try the simple way first.*

✐ *If you use a ceramic baking dish, it may take longer to bake the apples since it doesn't conduct the heat as well as glass.*

✐ *For a more elaborate dish, try this eighteenth-century idea: bird's nest pudding. Use a ceramic dish that holds the apples snugly. Fill the apple holes with raisins and chopped walnuts. Make a plain vanilla custard (beat 2 large eggs with an extra egg yolk just to blend; stir in ¼ cup sugar, a dash of salt, and 1½ cups milk. Stir well and add 1½ teaspoons pure vanilla extract. Pour through a strainer and then pour it around the apples). Grate some nutmeg over the top and sprinkle on a few more chopped walnuts. Bake at 350° for 1 hour or until the apples are soft and the custard is set (test with a knife). Serve with a dollop of sweetened whipped cream flavored with vanilla.*

✐ SAVORY BAKED APPLES: *If you're roasting pork, add apples to the pan 45 minutes before the pork is done. Core them and fill with grated horseradish.*

# Strawberry Shortcake

This dish is one of the great American contributions to culinary history—home cooking at its best. Make it only when you have ripe local strawberries or use raspberries.

People sometimes shy away from making their own shortcake, but it's very easy even though it involves a few seconds of kneading. Once you make these biscuits, you'll make them every summer just for the shortcake. The recipe comes from James Beard's childhood, a specialty of his family's Chinese cook.

*Serves 12*

2 cups flour

1 teaspoon salt

1 tablespoon baking powder

2 teaspoons sugar

¾ to 1 cup heavy cream as needed

Melted butter as needed

sweetened whipped cream for serving

2 pints strawberries

sugar to taste

Preheat the oven to 425°.

Sift the dry ingredients together into a bowl, whisk to mix, and fold in the cream until it makes a soft dough that can be handled easily. Turn out the dough onto a floured work surface and knead for about a minute. Pat the dough out to a thickness of about ¾ inch and cut into rounds or squares. Dip the biscuits in melted butter and arrange them on a buttered baking sheet. Bake for 15 to 18 minutes, until golden brown.

Rinse and dry the strawberries, then hull them. If they're very large, cut them in half. Mash a few of the berries to make them juicy.

While the biscuits are hot, split them and butter each side. Spoon a little sugar over the butter. Place them open-faced on a serving dish or in individual bowls and ladle the strawberries over. Let guests add their own sweetened whipped cream—a little pure vanilla extract and a little freshly grated nutmeg in the whipped cream will be much appreciated.

*Try making a big shortcake: Pat the biscuit dough into a big circle and bake it. When it's done, split it horizontally using a bread knife and add the butter and sugar. Spoon half the strawberries over the bottom layer, put the top layer on, and cover with the remaining strawberries. Cut the shortcake into wedges to serve and pass the whipped cream separately.*

# Oatmeal Cookies

hese homiest of all cookies are a snap to make and they always seem to disappear first on a cookie tray. This version is crisp and crunchy and keeps very well. The
nutmeg isn't always used in oatmeal cookies, but it adds an extra flavor that enhances
all the others while tasting just right, as though it were a classic combination. You
can add a pinch of ginger too, but then you're drifting off in the direction of spice
cookies and away from the simple goodness of oatmeal.

*Makes about 3 dozen cookies*

1½ cups flour

¼ teaspoon salt

1 teaspoon baking soda

1 scant teaspoon ground cinnamon

¼ teaspoon freshly grated nutmeg

½ pound (2 sticks) butter at room
   temperature

½ cup granulated sugar

1 cup packed light brown sugar

1 large egg

1 tablespoon milk

2 teaspoons pure vanilla extract

1½ cups old-fashioned oats
   (not instant)

¾ cup broken pecans or walnuts

½ cup raisins, plumped in hot water
   for 5 minutes and drained
   (optional)

Preheat the oven to 375°. Mix the flour, salt, baking soda, and spices in a bowl
and set aside. In a mixer or by hand, beat the butter with the sugars until the mixture
is creamy and light. Add the egg, milk, and vanilla and beat until mixed thoroughly.
Mix in the flour mixture well and stir in the oats, nuts, and drained raisins.

Drop by tablespoons onto an ungreased cookie sheet about 2 inches apart. Bake
for 12 minutes or until golden brown at the edges. Remove the cookie sheet from the
oven and let the cookies sit for a minute, then transfer to a rack to cool.

## Mini-Cheesecakes

*These tiny cheesecakes are made in little foil candy cups, perfect for a sweet-meat tray, or in small foil cupcake cups for a quickie dessert. Line the bottoms with a layer of cookie or graham cracker crumbs or, for the larger size, just drop in a superthin whole cookie like the Swedish ginger cookie or the all-American chocolate wafer. For filling 45 2-inch cups: Beat together three 8-ounce packages of Philadelphia cream cheese, ⅔ cup sugar, 3 large eggs, 2 teaspoons pure vanilla extract, and the grated zest of a lemon. Fill the cups, leaving about ¼ inch at the top for puffing. Preheat the oven to 350° and bake for 15 minutes. Pretty with a dot of sour cream and a single fresh berry on top.*

*A little fuss here will give you some excellent taste dividends: Toast the oats for 10 minutes in a 350° oven on a baking sheet; toast the nuts at the same temperature for about 7 minutes or until they smell good.*

*Keep the cookies well sealed, and they'll stay crisp.*

*For a softer cookie, mix in a tablespoon of vegetable shortening along with the butter.*

*Add a cupful of semisweet chocolate chips and you have cowboy cookies.*

CLASSIC AMERICAN FOOD WITHOUT FUSS

# Index

# About the Authors

FRANCES McCULLOUGH is a well-known book editor who specializes in cookbooks and literary works. She is a faculty member of the annual food writing course for professionals taught at the Culinary Institute of America at Greystone in the Napa Valley. She was the first recipient of the Roger Klein Award for Creative Editing.

BARBARA WITT is a cookbook author and restaurant consultant specializing in concepts, design, and menu development. She is also well known in Washington, D.C., and Baltimore as the former owner and operator of the nationally acclaimed Big Cheese restaurants.